Let's all draw

CATS

dogs and other animals

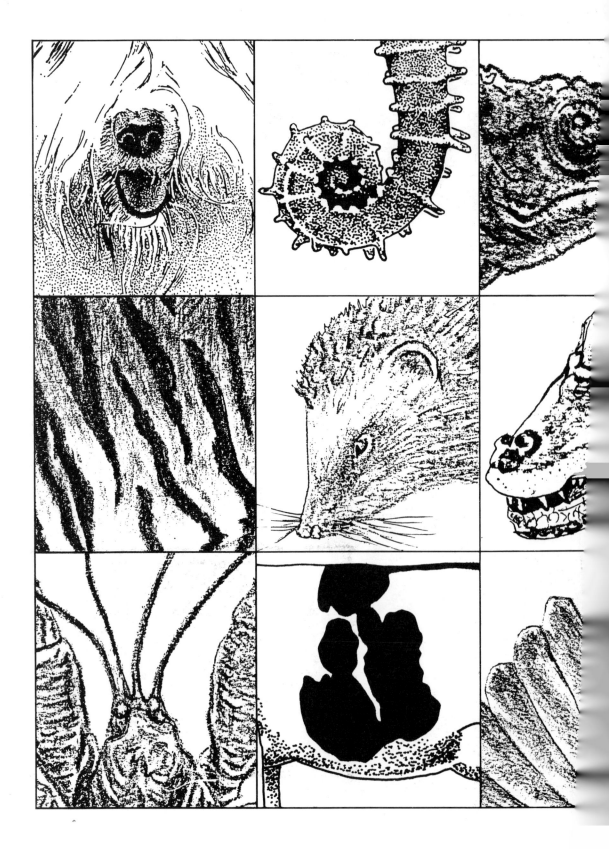

Here and at the back of the book are details
from some of the drawings featured. Can
you find the pages on which they appear?

Also in this series:

LET'S ALL DRAW CARS
trucks and other vehicles

LET'S ALL DRAW DINOSAURS
pterodactyls and other prehistoric creatures

LET'S ALL DRAW MONSTERS
ghosts, ghouls and demons

Illustrations by
Darren Bennett, James Dallas, Ryozo Kohira,
Kathleen McDougall, Bruce Robertson, Jane Robertson,
Graham Rosewarne, Tim Scrivens, Dino Skeete

© Diagram Visual Information Ltd 1990

First published in 1991 in the United States by Watson-
Guptill Publications, a division of BPI Communications,
Inc., 1515 Broadway, New York, New York 10036.

Library of Congress Cataloging-in-Publication Data

Robertson, Jane, 1965–
    Let's all draw cats, dogs, and other animals/Jane Robertson;
    text by Sue Pinkus.
      p.   cm. – (Let's all draw)
    Summary: Provides step-by-step instructions for drawing a variety
of animals.
      ISBN 0-8230-2705-8 (paper)
      1. Animals in art – Juvenile literature. 2. Drawing – Technique –
Juvenile literature. [1. Animals in art. 2. Drawing – Technique.]
I. Pinkus, Sue. II. Title. III. Series.
NC780. R6 1991
743'. 6 – dc20   90-40046
                                                             CIP
                                                             AC

Typeset by Bournetype, Bournemouth, England
Printed and bound by Snoeck Ducaju & Sons, Ghent, Belgium

1 2 3 4 5 / 96 95 94 93 92 91

Let's all draw
CATS
dogs and other animals

JANE ROBERTSON
Text by Sue Pinkus

WATSON-GUPTILL PUBLICATIONS/NEW YORK

About this book

Sketching animals is tremendous fun –
particularly if you can draw them from real life,
taking careful note of how they move, feed and
lie down.

Pages 8–19

THE ANIMAL KINGDOM

First, in **Part 1**, take a look at some of the
thousands of different creatures that make
up the animal kingdom. What is a reptile,
for instance? And which animals are
mammals? Read this section and find out.
(A few animals have names that are hard to
say. So we sometimes give you clues in this
book to help with this.)

Pages 20–49

GETTING READY TO DRAW

In **Part 2**, find out all you need to know
about using pencils, felt-tips, ballpoint
pens, crayons, brushes, paints and other
tools so that you can begin drawing animals
like a true wildlife artist.

In this book, you will find lots of step-by-step drawings to copy. As you do more drawings, you will find you can use lines more freely. You can rub out your first rough sketch lines if you wish, but you can also leave them in, as many artists do.

As you can see, this book has large page numbers. They are there to help you find your way easily to a drawing you might need to look at again while you are working.

Pages 50–67

DRAWING ANIMALS IS EASY!

Part 3 explores the way you can start making amazing animal pictures easily, step-by-step. Begin with just a few basic shapes. It won't be long before you are a sketching a fabulous tiger like the one on pages 106–107.

Pages 68–139

YOUR ANIMAL GALLERY

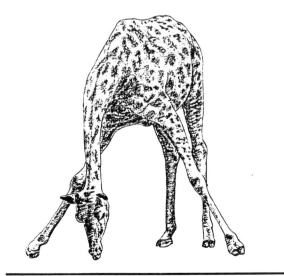

In **Part 4**, there's a whole animal gallery for you to look at and copy – a penguin, a giraffe, an elephant, a tortoise, a zebra, a loris, a parrot and lots of other creatures, too. There are expert hints and special tips as well. By now you'll be well on your way to making some fantastic drawings!

Part 1

Some animals live in the sea and swim. Others
have wings and fly, or crawl about. Some are
found in the jungle. Others live in the desert, or
in polar regions. Some are fierce – like bears
and leopards. Others are tame and often kept
as pets – cats and rabbits, for instance.

THE ANIMAL KINGDOM

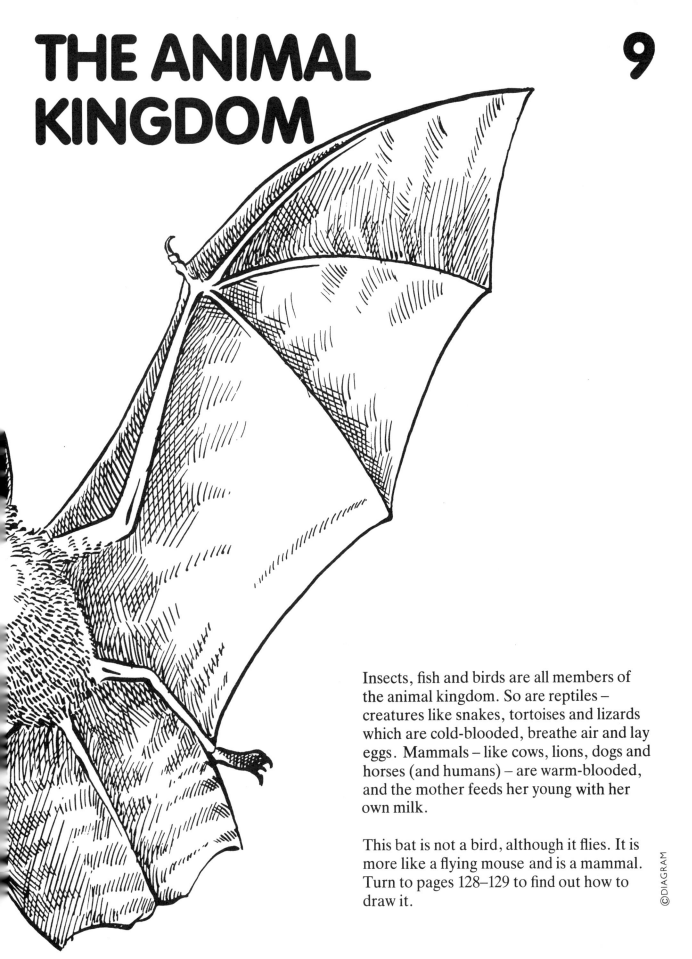

Insects, fish and birds are all members of the animal kingdom. So are reptiles – creatures like snakes, tortoises and lizards which are cold-blooded, breathe air and lay eggs. Mammals – like cows, lions, dogs and horses (and humans) – are warm-blooded, and the mother feeds her young with her own milk.

This bat is not a bird, although it flies. It is more like a flying mouse and is a mammal. Turn to pages 128–129 to find out how to draw it.

©DIAGRAM

Cats' cousins

Caterpillars and kittens are cousins. They both are animals and, like you and I, need food, light, air and water to live.

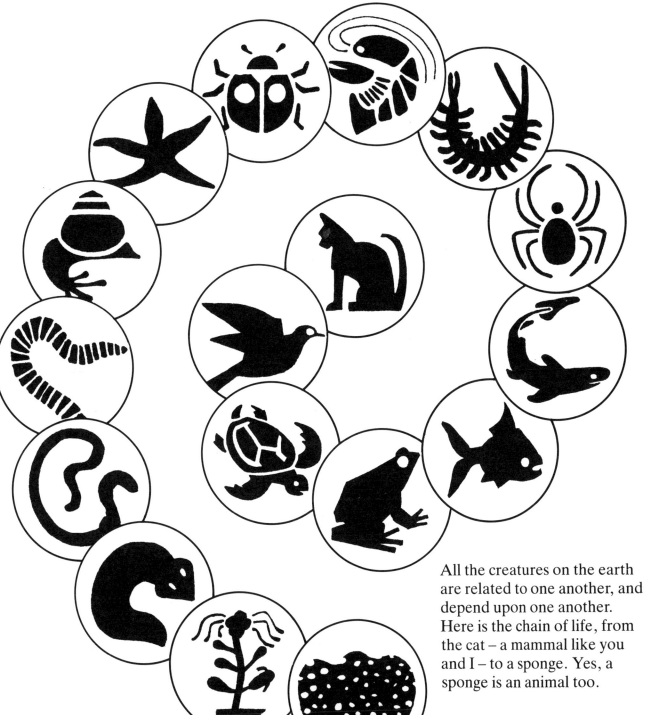

All the creatures on the earth are related to one another, and depend upon one another. Here is the chain of life, from the cat – a mammal like you and I – to a sponge. Yes, a sponge is an animal too.

The long, the short and the tall

Here are ten different animals, shown by the side of an adult man and woman so that you can get an idea of their size. Can you name them all? (Check your answers with those given upside down on the page opposite.)

The tallest is the giraffe, which is more than three times the size of a full-grown human being. Do you know where giraffes live in the wild? Turn to page 102 if you are not sure. And where in the world – apart from on pages 116–117 – might you meet an armadillo?

Further on in the book you will find step-by-step guides to drawing four more of the creatures shown here.

Three of the creatures shown are often ridden by people, and you might find three of them on a farm. Which are they?

This giant, hairy, bird-eating spider from South America has been drawn life-size. Have you ever seen a spider as large as this? Take a piece of tracing paper and draw around your hand with a pencil. Now put the tracing paper over the spider on this page. He's even bigger than your hand, isn't he? And he's much bigger, too, than the tiny creature in the corner. It's called a shrew (say *shroo*), and has also been drawn life-size.

Here are the answers to the quiz on page 12.

1 Giraffe   2 Elephant   3 Horse
4 Ostrich   5 Cow   6 Camel
7 Bear   8 Armadillo   9 Cat
10 Rhinoceros

© DIAGRAM

People and animals

Most people are fond of animals, and many of them keep pets. How many different sorts of pets can you name? Here's a start: dogs, cats, rabbits, canaries...

Once you start drawing animals, you can ask your friends and relatives if you can sketch their pets when you visit them.

If you ever visit a farm, you will find many different types of animals there, too – pigs cows, sheep, turkeys and hens perhaps, and maybe even a goat. All are raised by the farmer for the food they give – eggs, milk or meat. But some also provide material for clothing. Do you know which they are?

You can also find lots of wild creatures in the garden if you have one, or in the countryside – squirrels, owls, swans, butterflies and insects. And there will be more exotic creatures, too, from all over the world at a zoo or safari park.

Cats live in all three places: the home, where they are pets; on farms, where they work by catching the mice and rats that eat the farmers' corn; and in the wild, as lions, tigers and leopards, for instance, which also belong to the cat family.

In the home

On the farm

In the wild

Animals as pets

You will probably find it easy to get to look at lots of cats and dogs because there are so many that are kept as pets. But perhaps you also know someone who has a really unusual pet, like a monkey or a snake.

Some people have pets that come from far corners of the world. Parrots, for example, live in the jungle in countries like Brazil. They can often be taught to talk, but they probably don't understand a word!

Some people keep mice. Those sold in pet shops are very friendly and are not like the mice that carry diseases and destroy food in your kitchen.

Some tortoises come from desert areas but many live near water. In our winters, they hibernate (say *high-burn-eight*). This means that they go to sleep for a few months until there are signs that spring is on its way.

A sea horse, kept in a tank, might come from the coasts along the west shore of the Atlantic Ocean. It is important that the tank is kept at the right temperature, and that they are also fed the right amount – not too much and not too little.

Which sort of pet would you like to have if you were given a choice? They all need caring for, feeding and perhaps grooming or taking for walks, remember. It is important to look after a pet properly.

© DIAGRAM

Different breeds

All cats have four legs, but although many are fluffy, others are smooth. Some are brown or white; others are black, and a few may even be a shade of blue, while some have interesting markings. This is because there are lots of different types or breeds of cat, as you will see if you ever go to a cat show.

On these two pages you can see five different types of cats.

1 This is a long-haired Persian, which is very soft to stroke.
2 This cat has a thin tail, a smooth body and long legs. It is a crossbreed, which means that its father was a different type of cat from its mother.
3 This Siamese cat has a pale body and darker face, ears, tail and legs. It has beautiful blue eyes.
4 This tabby cat has markings all over its body and short hair. It is one of the most popular of all breeds of cat.
5 This long-haired Persian cat is black and white, and has orange-brown eyes.

1

2

Can you name twelve breeds of dog? Here are a few to start you off: poodle, dalmatian, corgi, cocker spaniel…

3

4

5

Part 2

What sort of paper is it best to draw on? How can you use pencils, crayons, ink or paint to get different effects? You'll find the answers to these and many other questions about drawing in this part of your book.

GETTING READY TO DRAW

It is not just important to have the right paper and tools to make good animal pictures. You need to take care over them as you work, too. So don't rush your drawings. Take your time.

Why not start an animal scrapbook, too, by cutting out interesting wildlife pictures from magazines and newspapers? It will be a helpful reference book once you start drawing. Here is a page from my elephant scrapbook.

©DIAGRAM

Good places to draw

Before you get started, take a little time to choose the space you are going to work in. Get everything ready, too.

Would you like to spend time drawing with a friend? Or would you prefer to draw on your own? Make up your mind before you begin.

Working on the floor can be fun. It will also give you lots of space so that you can lay out all the pencils, paints, pens and paper you need. (But make sure that any rug or carpet on the floor is covered with old newspaper or a plastic sheet before you start.) If you work on the floor, you will need to stand up from time to time to take a good look at your drawings.

Have a hard surface like a board or a piece of cardboard on which to put the paper you will be using. It will be best, too, if the paper is not so large that you need to lean on it to reach a far corner.

Working on a table is sometimes a bit easier, as you can get really close to your drawings when you lean forward.

Wherever you choose to work, make sure you have plenty of light. By a window may be best. If you are right-handed, try to sit so that the light from a window or a lamp comes over your left shoulder. If you are left-handed, try to arrange things so that the light comes over your right shoulder.

Reminders:

- Think about what you would like to draw before you start.
- Decide whether you will use a ballpoint, crayons, pencil, felt-tips, chalks or paints. Or perhaps ink?
- How large will your drawing be? Plan it so that it will fit the paper.
- Try not to hurry your drawing. You can always come back to it later if someone calls you away.

Which tools for different effects?

These pictures are taken from three different drawings that appear elsewhere in this book. Can you tell what they were drawn with? Find them in the book to see if you are right. (The pages to turn to are shown by each whole drawing.)

The first picture in each row, going across these two pages, is part of the whole picture at the size it was drawn. The next picture is a detail from it, shown bigger. The third picture shows the whole drawing at a small size. Each has a different effect, doesn't it?

Before you start to draw, think about the sort of effect you would like. Do you need the creature to look soft and cuddly or rough-skinned? Would you like to be able to rub out any mistakes? Will you want to fill in large areas with skin markings or fur? The next few pages tell you whether you should choose pencils, crayons, felt-tips, paints or a ballpoint once you have decided what you want your drawing to look like.

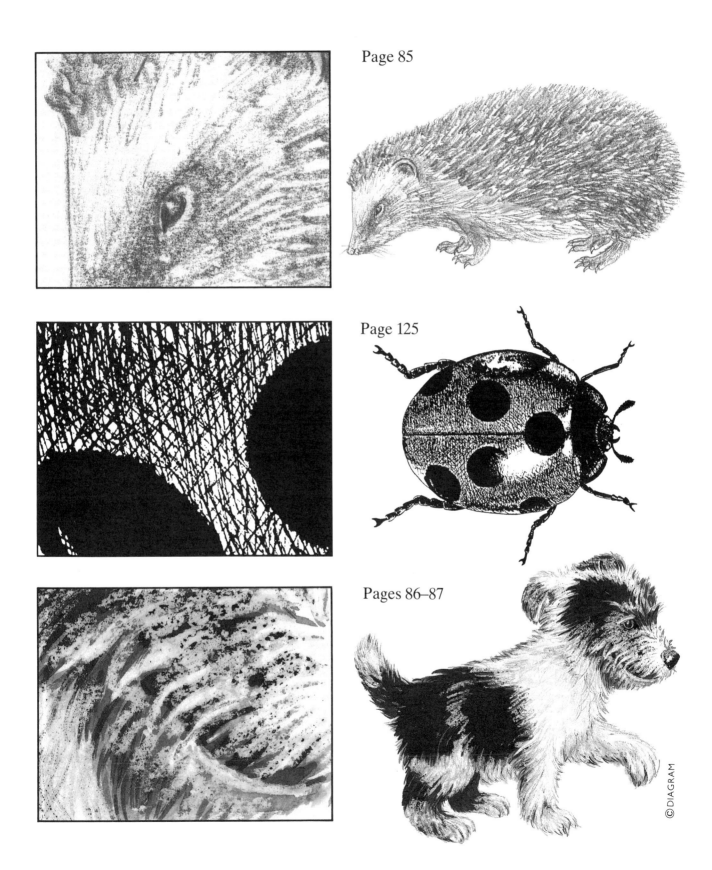

Page 85

Page 125

Pages 86–87

Drawing with pencils

Most people like drawing with pencils.
They are easy to use and can be rubbed out.
when you are planning a picture or if you
make a mistake.

When you buy a pencil, you'll see it has a
grade (a letter and perhaps a number, too)
on the side. If you would like to make
smudgy lines, look for grades B or 2B.
These are soft. For fine, hard lines, use a
pencil with an H or 2H grade. A soft pencil
is best for planning a drawing, as a B or 2B
pencil is easily rubbed out.

You can, of course, get pencils in lots of
different shades – with red, blue, green,
orange, yellow, brown or purple leads, for
example.

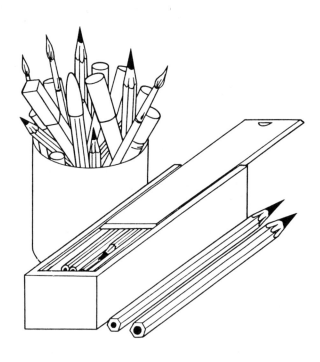

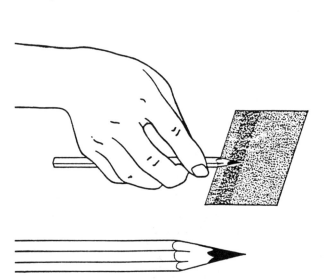

Always keep your pencils sharpened. There
should be just enough lead showing so that
the point will not snap when you work.
Rubbing the side of your pencil across a
sheet of glasspaper (sandpaper) will give it
a good point. Store pencils in a box or keep
them in a jar with their points upward.

Pencils work best on paper that has a rough
surface.

This is a soft (2B) pencil drawing of a very
handsome tabby cat. Look how different
the shape of its eyes are from those of the
Siamese cat on page 33. In the dark, the
central black areas, called the pupils, get
bigger. But when it is light, the pupils get
smaller.

Do you think this cat is sitting in sunshine or
shade?

Drawing with chalks and crayons

There are several different sorts of chalks and crayons. All of them will give your drawings lots of action, but they may smudge easily if you are not careful. Use paper with a rough surface for the best results.

1 Pastel sticks come in a large number of shades and are covered in paper so that your hands won't get grubby when you pick them up.

2 Pastel pencils work a bit like lead pencils but it is difficult to keep them sharp. This means that they are better for shading than for drawing.

3 Chalks give interesting textures but you cannot sharpen them.

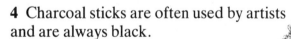

4 Charcoal sticks are often used by artists and are always black.

5 Wax crayons also come in lots of shades and different thicknesses. They are good for covering large areas but are often hard to rub out.

While you are drawing with chalks, crayons or charcoal, remember to rest your hand on a spare piece of paper so that you do not smudge your picture.

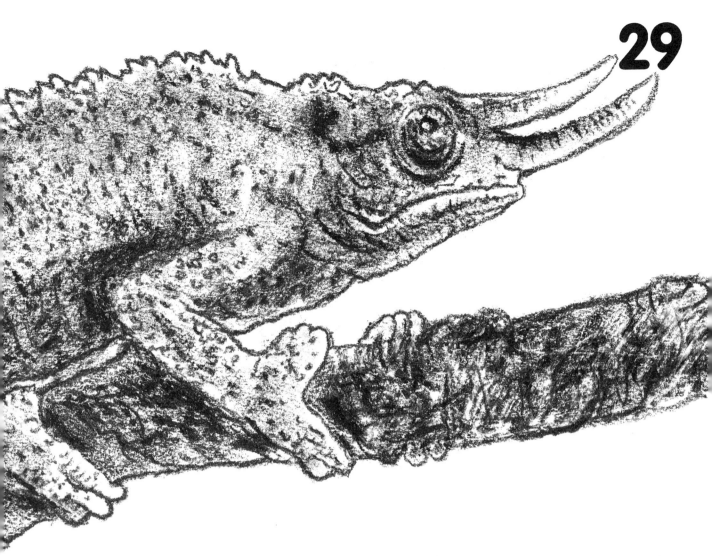

After drawing the outline of this chameleon (say *cam-eel-yon*), Paul placed the paper over his front doorstep and rubbed over it with a crayon to get the mottled effect of the creature's skin. You can find out more about making different sorts of textures in this way if you turn to pages 34–35.

Did you know that the chameleon – a small lizard – can change from green to brown or from yellow to red, in order to hide itself in its surroundings? Notice how big its eyes are, how sulky it looks and how its tail curls right around.

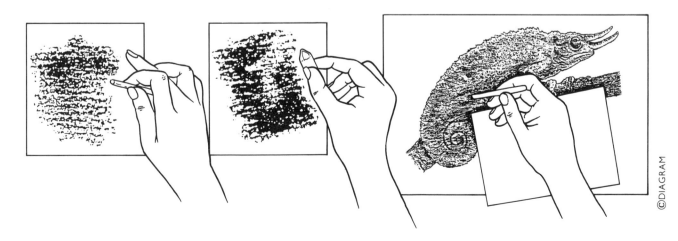

©DIAGRAM

Drawing with pens

Marks made with any sort of ink do not rub out easily. This means that if you decide to draw with ink, you need to do a pencil outline or rough sketch first before you begin your final picture. You can, of course, also trace, using ink.

Ink will not give you a chance to shade as you can when you use a pencil. So if you use a pen to do your drawing, you will have to build up darker areas in your picture with lots of dots or crisscross lines.

Remember to keep the tops on your felt-tips when you are not using them or the ink may dry up.

Try to keep ink off your hands while you are drawing or you may get blotches and fingermarks all over your pictures. Take care as well not to spill any ink if you are using a fountain pen or dip pen. And try not to get it on your clothes. It is sometimes such a problem to wash out.

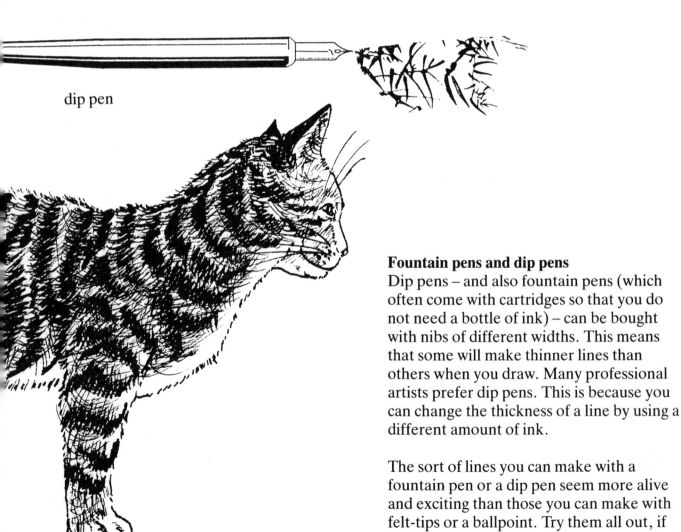

dip pen

Fountain pens and dip pens
Dip pens – and also fountain pens (which often come with cartridges so that you do not need a bottle of ink) – can be bought with nibs of different widths. This means that some will make thinner lines than others when you draw. Many professional artists prefer dip pens. This is because you can change the thickness of a line by using a different amount of ink.

The sort of lines you can make with a fountain pen or a dip pen seem more alive and exciting than those you can make with felt-tips or a ballpoint. Try them all out, if you can, and see the differences for yourself.

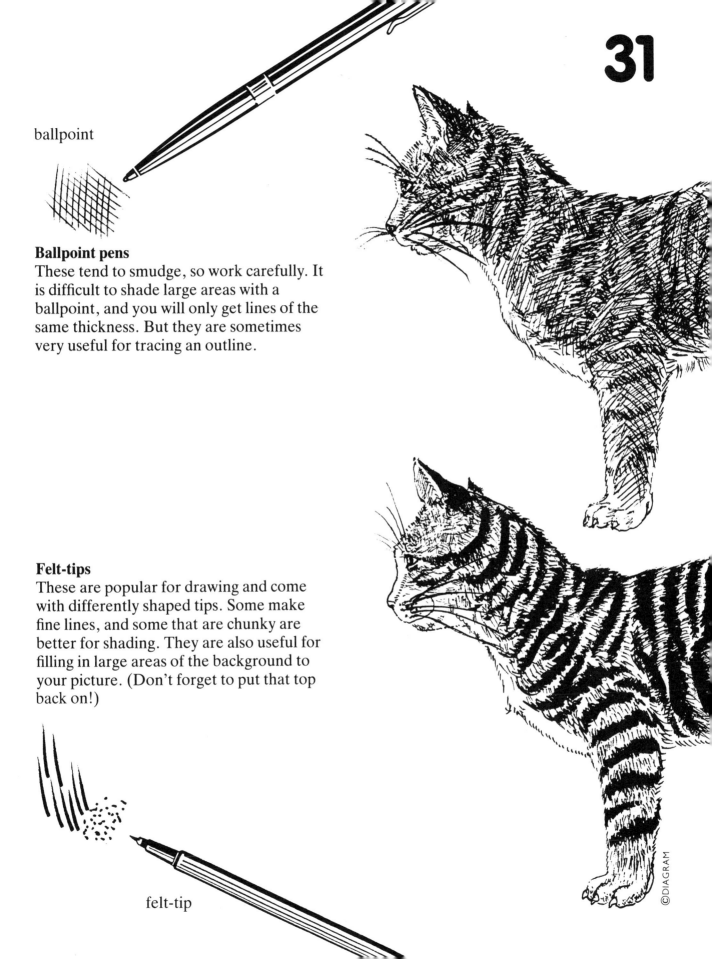

ballpoint

Ballpoint pens

These tend to smudge, so work carefully. It is difficult to shade large areas with a ballpoint, and you will only get lines of the same thickness. But they are sometimes very useful for tracing an outline.

Felt-tips

These are popular for drawing and come with differently shaped tips. Some make fine lines, and some that are chunky are better for shading. They are also useful for filling in large areas of the background to your picture. (Don't forget to put that top back on!)

felt-tip

©DIAGRAM

Using brushes

If you use a brush, this means you can water down your paint or ink to get lighter shades. You can give soft edges to your drawings, too.

Brushes come in different thicknesses. Large ones are good for filling in big areas. Fine ones are better for drawing lines. The very best brushes are made from sable or squirrel hair, but cheaper ones can be very good, too.

Use strong paper when you work with a brush. If you paint on very thin paper, your drawing may curl up.

As you paint, start with lighter tones and build them up into darker areas slowly. Wait until large areas are dry before you add detail with a pen or pencil.

Use your brushes gently. Don't put too much paint on them or you may get blotches everywhere.

Wash all your brushes after you have used them, and store them in a jar so that the brush ends point upward. This will prevent them from becoming damaged.

This Siamese cat is nursing her young. Use the step-by-step stages on pages 94–95 to help you draw her face; and turn to pages 88–89 if you would like to see some more playful kittens.

Making textures

Find a piece of sandpaper and run your hand over it. Rough, isn't it? Now try to find a piece of silk and run your hand over that. You can feel the difference.
What you are feeling is known as texture. The sandpaper and the silk look very different and they also have a different sort of texture when you run your fingers over them.

Giving the effect of texture to your drawings, so that you can almost feel what it would be like to stroke a tiger, is easier than you may think. There are lots of ways to do it, as you will see.

To experiment with texture, I suggest you try out everything on scraps of paper first.

Smudge it!
If you work on strong paper with pencils or chalks, you can rub or smudge parts of your drawing using a finger or a tissue – not by accident but on purpose – to get a soft effect.

Rub it!
If you draw on thin paper, after you have finished your outline, place it over a rough surface (a piece of wood or some fabric perhaps) and then rub crayon across the area you want to cover. This will give you a texture like the wood or fabric that you put under the paper.

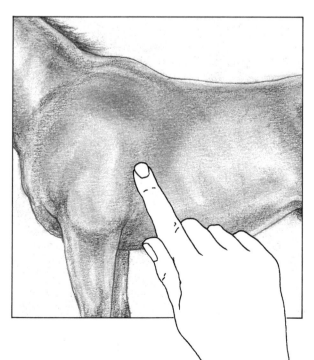

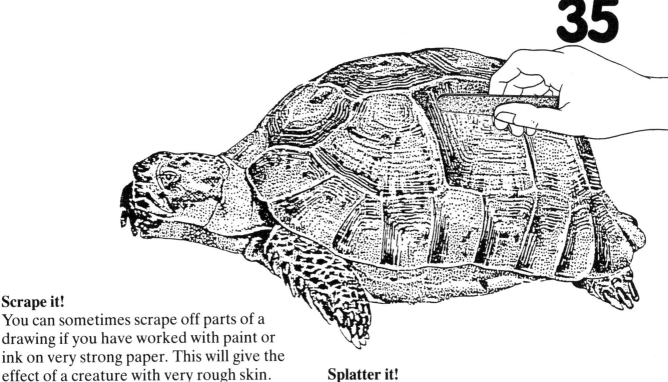

Scrape it!

You can sometimes scrape off parts of a drawing if you have worked with paint or ink on very strong paper. This will give the effect of a creature with very rough skin. You can use a nail file for this.

Dab it!

If you work with a pen and ink, you can carefully dab the edges of your drawing with a wet tissue to give a softer effect. Be sure to work with strong paper if you would like to try this out or the wet tissue may make a hole in it.

Splatter it!

This is fun! When you have finished the outline of the creature you are drawing, cut it out and put it on some old newspaper. Find an old toothbrush that you are sure no one wants any more. Dip the brush into ink or paint and splatter a spray at the drawing, flicking off the paint or ink gently with a small stick. (It is best to put something over your clothes when you do this.)

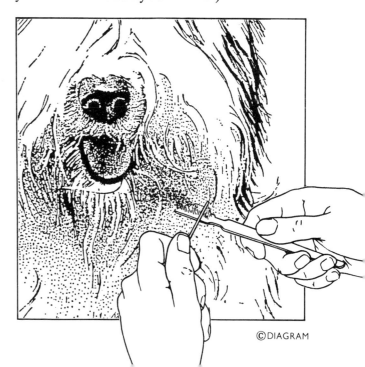

©DIAGRAM

Special effects

Some paints and inks are water-soluble. This means they will dissolve in water. If you use soluble paints, you will find that they do not cover marks that have been made with wax crayons. There are some very exciting special effects you can get in this way.

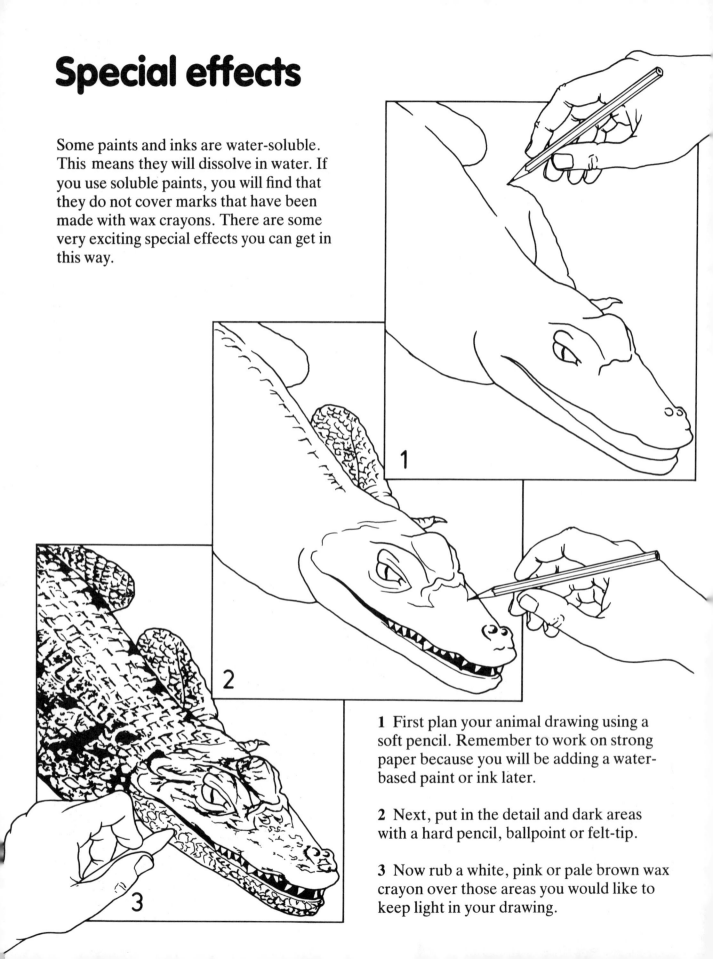

1 First plan your animal drawing using a soft pencil. Remember to work on strong paper because you will be adding a water-based paint or ink later.

2 Next, put in the detail and dark areas with a hard pencil, ballpoint or felt-tip.

3 Now rub a white, pink or pale brown wax crayon over those areas you would like to keep light in your drawing.

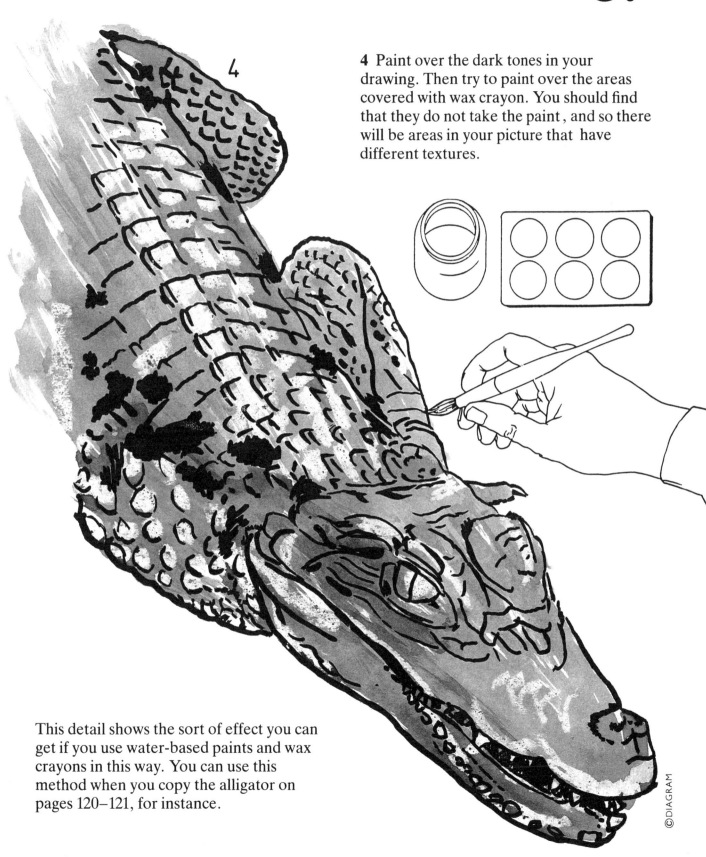

4 Paint over the dark tones in your drawing. Then try to paint over the areas covered with wax crayon. You should find that they do not take the paint , and so there will be areas in your picture that have different textures.

This detail shows the sort of effect you can get if you use water-based paints and wax crayons in this way. You can use this method when you copy the alligator on pages 120–121, for instance.

©DIAGRAM

Choosing paper

The sort of paper you should use depends on whether you are working with a pencil, inks or paint. If you use very thin paper, for example, you cannot work with paints as the paper may curl up.

If you use thick paper, you cannot trace a drawing. But you could transfer a tracing on to thick paper using the method described on pages 40–41.

Tracing paper
It is always useful to have some thin paper that you can see through. This will be helpful because you can learn a lot by tracing pictures of animals, birds, fish and insects from books. You can also trace drawings you have already made.

Looking after your paper
A lot of people throw away good paper that you might use for drawing. If someone in your family does this, see if you can rescue it. Even small pieces are useful for rough sketches. Save them until next time you draw.

Keep all your drawing paper flat. But if it comes in a roll, simply roll it back the other way to stop it from curling up again.

Always work with clean hands. This will help you to avoid horrid fingermarks all over your work.

Points to remember about paper

- Tracing paper is very useful if you want to copy drawings from books. You can also use it to transfer drawings onto cardboard or thick paper. But you cannot use a paintbrush on tracing paper very well.
- Smooth paper is usually good for felt-tips. But it is not very strong, so it is best not to use water-paints on this sort of paper.
- Some papers, which you can buy in an art shop and come in lots of different shades other than white, will usually take paint.
- Strong drawing paper is also sold in art shops and wil! usually have a rough surface. This means it is good for pencils, inks and paints.
- The thickness of a paper is called its weight. So when you buy paper, you can ask for a heavyweight or lightweight sort.

Drawing pads

You can buy paper in single sheets at an art shop. But you can also buy drawing pads. These are often a good idea as it means you can keep all your pictures together in one place.

Tracing

Sometimes it can help to trace an outline of an animal from a book. You can then add your own shading.

Choose a picture that has a bold shape so that you do not get confused about which lines to follow on the tracing paper. A pencil will usually be best for tracing, but you can also use a ballpoint or a felt-tip.

You can trace any picture in this book. To help you start, here is a picture of a horse and a foal, drawn from the side. Simply follow the clear outline, using a sharp pencil or fine felt-tip or ballpoint.

If you would like to transfer a tracing onto another piece of paper or cardboard, you can easily do this using the following method.

First cover the picture with clear tracing paper and fix this to the page with the sort of tape that peels off without leaving a mark. This is usually called masking tape. Do not use ordinary sticky tape – it will damage the book.

Using a sharp pencil, now draw round the main shape. You can also trace any of the details you think it may be hard to copy later, if you like.

Now remove the tracing paper. Turn it over, and rub with the side of a soft pencil (grade B) on to the lines that show through to the back of the tracing paper.

Turn the tracing paper back again to its right side. Now put it on a piece of paper or cardboard. This time, use a hard pencil (grade 2H) with a sharp point, and go over all the lines quite firmly.

When you take the tracing paper away, you should find you have a shadow of the drawing on the paper or card beneath it. You can use these ghost lines as part of your own drawing.

Remember not to press too hard when you trace as you may spoil the picture you are copying.

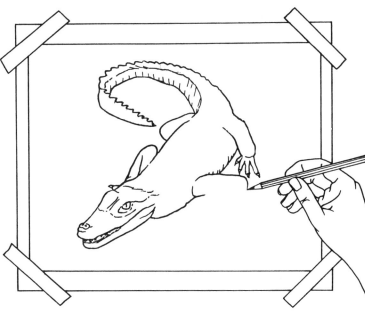

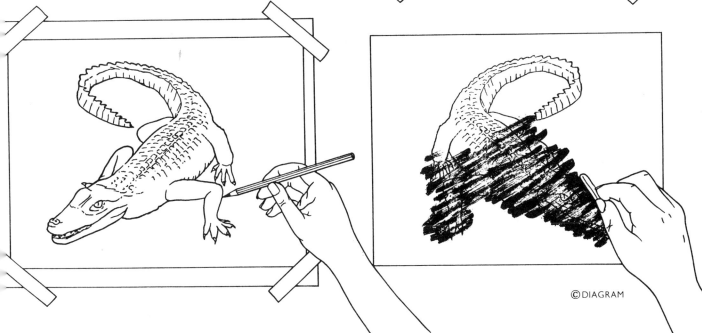

©DIAGRAM

Copying

Copying

Copying drawings will give you lots of ideas for your own pictures. Try hard to get the shapes right or your copy will not look like the original. Of course, if you use a pencil and the original was done in ink, the two will be very different. One drawing will look softer than the other. Here are some useful tips to help you master the art of copying.

Plan your drawing

Using a soft pencil, draw the basic shape first before you try to fill in any details. If you look at the rough sketch of the cat below, for instance, you can see how its head fits into a square shape. Its body, as it sits, is more than twice the height of its head and fits into a rectangle, with only the tummy and back legs sticking out. How many paws can be seen?

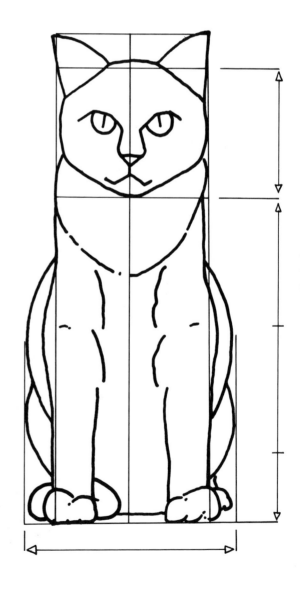

Here is a very pretty tabby cat for you to copy. Before you start, try to think of it fitting into a simple framework of one small square for the head, and one larger rectangle for the body.

Keep checking your drawing
When you are copying, keep looking back at the original drawing to check you are putting everything in the right place. (Where is the tail? And where do the whiskers start?)

Making drawings bigger

It is easy to change the size of your drawing or any picture you are copying from a book by using squares.

First turn the picture you are copying upside down so that the top of the animal is at the bottom of the page. This will help you to concentrate when you copy the outline.

Now trace your drawing or a picture in a book. Next, draw squares over your tracing, as shown, using a ruler for straight lines. Make sure all the lines are the same distance apart. First draw them across your tracing paper and then down the paper.

Now take a larger sheet of paper and again draw squares, but this time make the squares larger than those on the tracing paper. Take care that you draw the same number of squares. If there are 24 squares on your tracing paper, there must be 24 larger squares on the larger piece of paper.

Next, copy the tracing onto the other sheet of paper, matching carefully what is in each square. For example, the third square from the left at the top of the tracing paper should match the third square from the left at the top of your drawing paper.

Watch where the lines of the picture cross each square on the tracing paper. Make them cross at exactly the same points on the larger squares on your drawing paper.

Then turn your paper right side up. You should have an exact copy of the original outline.

On page 140, there are some squares that you can trace with a pencil and ruler to use for enlarging in this way. You can enlarge the mouse (opposite) so that it is much bigger than the cat on page 43.

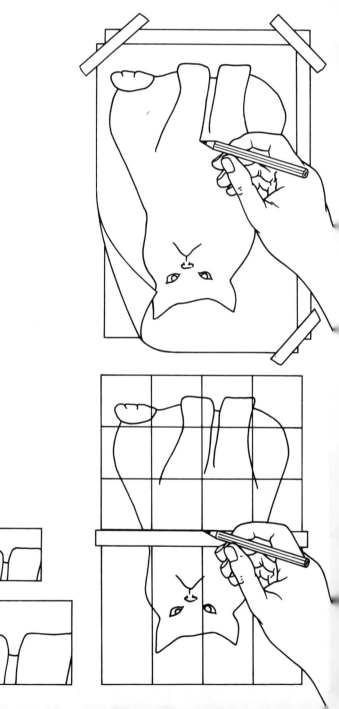

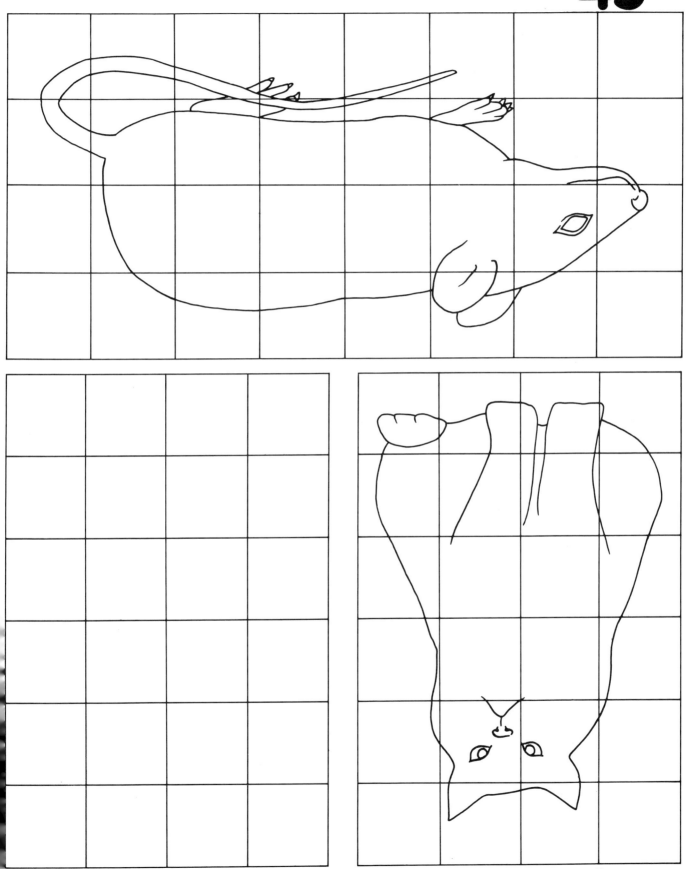

Using your drawings

There are lots of interesting things you can do with your drawings of animals when you have finished them. So try to think about how you would like to use your pictures before you start on them. Here are some ideas.

Try cutting out simple animal shapes and making them into mobiles to hang up with thread or wire. It will be best to draw on cardboard rather than on paper for this, and to get an adult to help you put up the mobile.

You can make a frieze by drawing rows of all different sorts of creatures along a roll of paper. Or you could draw some creatures on cardboard. Cut them out and use the shapes left as stencils. Using masking tape, fix the cut-out shapes left to the roll of paper and fill in the cut-out areas with a felt-tip or paint, as shown. You could then

put up this Noah's ark frieze on the wall of your room.

You could also use special fabric paints to make your own animal design on a T-shirt.

Cards are fun to make for birthdays or Christmas. If you are sending out party invitations, these could have a wildlife theme. There could be a drawing with a message underneath. Or you can make a folded card with a picture on the front and a written message inside. Make sure you have envelopes of the right size before you begin.

You could even make your own wildlife magazine about different animals which your friends and family might enjoy reading. Give it a name like 'Pet News' or 'Safari Weekly'.

Visit the library and bookshops, and try to find out all you can about the animal kingdom so that your text will be interesting and accurate.

If you would like to make cut-outs of animals that will stand up, remember to leave a small extra piece of cardboard at the bottom, as shown. If you bend part of this forward and part of it back, the creatures will keep upright. You could make a whole safari park, zoo or farmyard in this way.

©DIAGRAM

Crazy cats

It can be wonderful to make really good drawings of animals like cats. But why not try your hand at some crazy cartoon cats, too, like those shown here? Some are fat and some are thin; some look surprised, and some look angry. There's even one cross cat with a spider on his nose!

It can be fun to make a bookmark to help you keep your place in a book you are reading. Cut out a long strip of paper about the width of a ruler, and then draw a picture of a cat – or any other animal you like – on it. Bookmarks make very good presents.

Bookplates are an excellent idea, too. They are not what librarians eat from but labels you can decorate and put your name and address on before you glue them in the front of your books. This means that, if you have a book that goes astray, whoever finds it will know it belongs to you.

PETER BROWN
THE HILL FARM
CORK IRELAND

Jane Robins
13 West Avenue
London

©DIAGRAM

Part 3

In this part of the book you can find out how to start drawing animals using very simple shapes. The tabby cat shown here can be drawn in various ways.

1 You can begin by thinking of the head, body and legs as circles, triangles and ovals.
2 Then you can join them up to make a silhouette.
3 You can also add fur texture.
4 Or you might begin with a stick creature, like the one shown here.
5 You could also draw a skeleton. The bones of a cat's skeleton move just like ours when we jump or turn round. So think about the position of a cat's bones if you draw it leaping, running or lying down.

DRAWING ANIMALS IS EASY!

6 Remember that cats – like all other creatures – are not flat like a piece of paper but solid and with depth, like a coffee pot. Thinking of a cat or other animal as a tin-can creature will help your drawings look more lifelike.

Simple shapes

If you want to draw a difficult creature, it is usually much easier to think of the shapes of its parts. Most animals can be drawn by putting together simple shapes like circles, ovals, diamonds and triangles.

This beetle is simply an oval with six sausage shapes for legs. The caterpillar is made from circles, triangles and a diamond. The rabbit has a large oval for its body, a smaller one for its head and triangles for ears. The bat next to it has two big triangles for wings, with the rest of its body made from an oval, a circle and three more triangles.

On this page, a mouse, bird, cat and horse have all been drawn using a few basic shapes in the same way. Which is which?

Try copying each of these creatures, and then shade in the shapes using crayons or felt-tips.

Animal shapes

It is often easiest to draw an animal from the side. This is because details which show what it is like are more easily recognized from the side than from other views.

When you start your picture, forget about the complicated patterns and textures and look very carefully at the basic shape and the outline.

When you have drawn the outline, you can then fill in the body using a felt-tip or thick crayon to make a flat shape called a silhouette.

You know what the two animals are on this page, but you will probably find it a bit of a problem to recognize some of those on the next page.

After guessing what each animal is, check your answers by looking at pages 73, 78–79, 91, 92, 109, 115 and 135

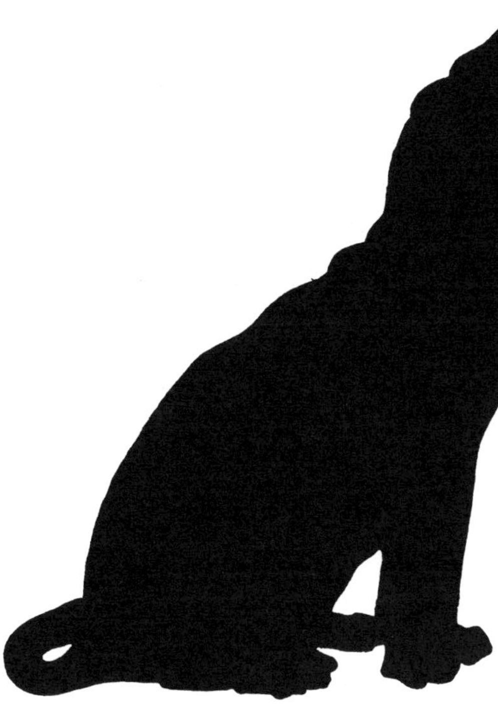

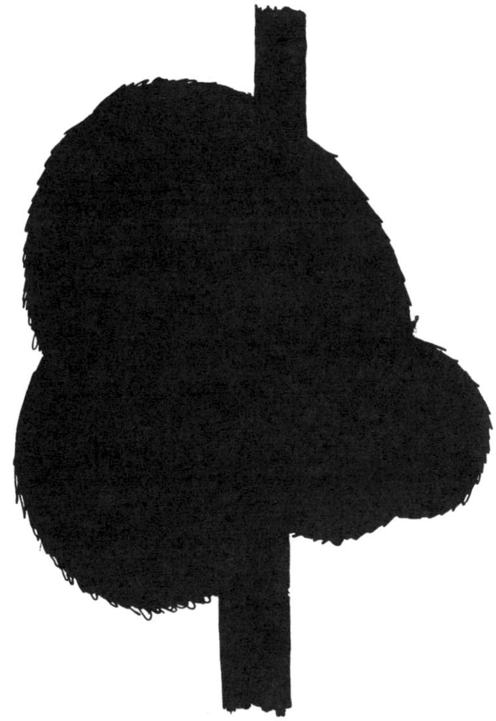

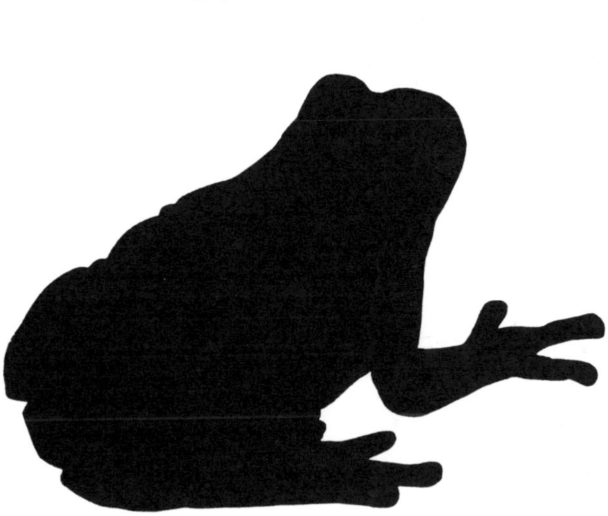

Patterned or plain?

Tabby

Some cats have very long, shaggy hair. Others are smooth-bodied. Some are all one shade – brown, black, white or ginger. Others have markings on their fur, like three of the four on this page.

When you are drawing a cat, you will need to think about whether any markings cover its whole body or are on just part of it.

Siamese

Patchy

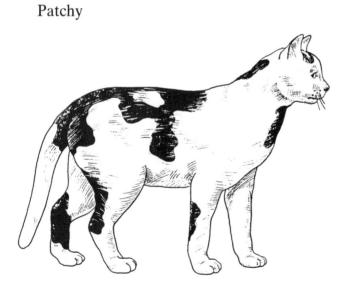

Tortoiseshell

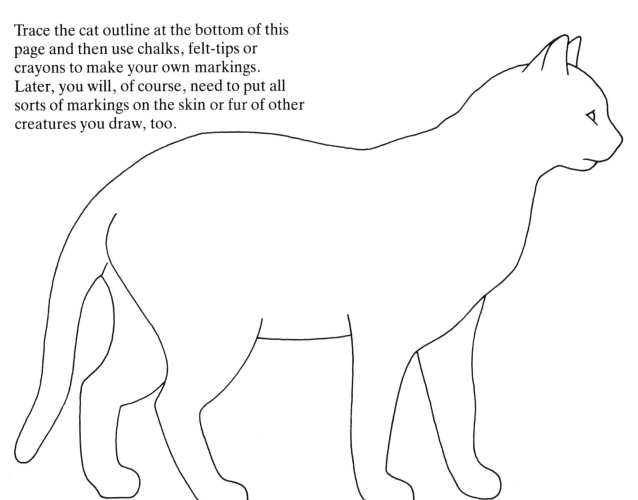

Cats' coats are long-haired and fluffy or short-haired and smooth – or a little of both.

Trace the cat outline at the bottom of this page and then use chalks, felt-tips or crayons to make your own markings. Later, you will, of course, need to put all sorts of markings on the skin or fur of other creatures you draw, too.

©DIAGRAM

Stick creatures

When you move, the various parts of your body stay the same shape. But as you bend your arms and knees when running or walking, the shape of your body as a whole changes. This is true of animals, too.

All creatures have a way of keeping their balance when they move. Some, for example, have long tails to help with this. Those that run fast have legs that move easily.

People have various points in their bodies where they can bend – elbows, wrists, necks, knees, shoulders and hips. Lots of animals have joints like these, too.

On these two pages you can see several animals drawn to look as if they are made from sticks. There's a rabbit, giraffe, frog, crab and horse – all drawn as stick creatures. Can you tell which is which?

Try copying them. Then, once you have mastered the idea, try to sketch an elephant or a tiger as stick figures, too. When you plan a drawing of a moving stick creature, try putting a series of dots where you think the joints should be. You can then copy the drawing but move the legs or arms from the points where you put the dots that mark the joints.

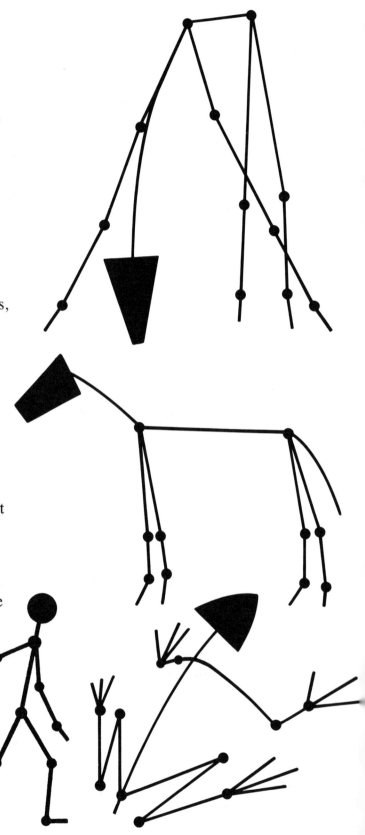

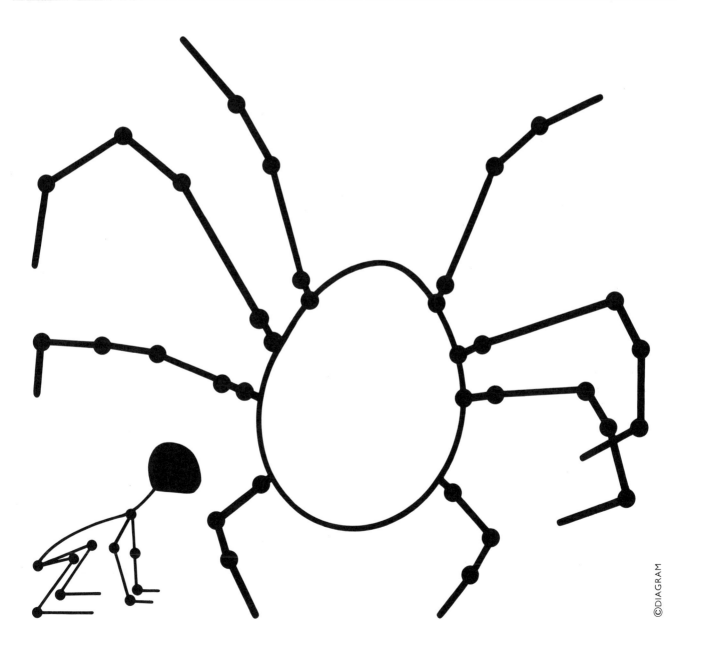

On the move

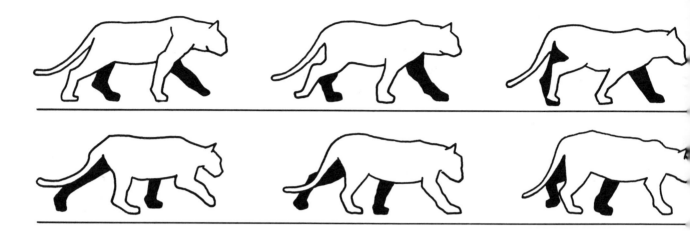

Cats prowl, walk, climb, run and leap. It is fascinating to watch them move.

Here are lots of drawings of cats in action for you to copy. But it is also a good idea to spend some time watching a cat on the move next time you see one.

In the drawings at the top of these two pages, I have shaded the cat's left legs black so that it is easy to see where they are as it walks along.

When you draw any four-legged animal on the move, at least two of its legs should always be on the ground – unless, of course, it is leaping.

If you would like to make an animal look as if it is really moving, fasten together twelve small pieces of thick paper with a staple or two to make a little book. Then draw each of the cats below on a separate right hand page. Now flick the pages quickly. The effect will be to make the cat seem to run. This is how artists draw moving creatures in cartoon films.

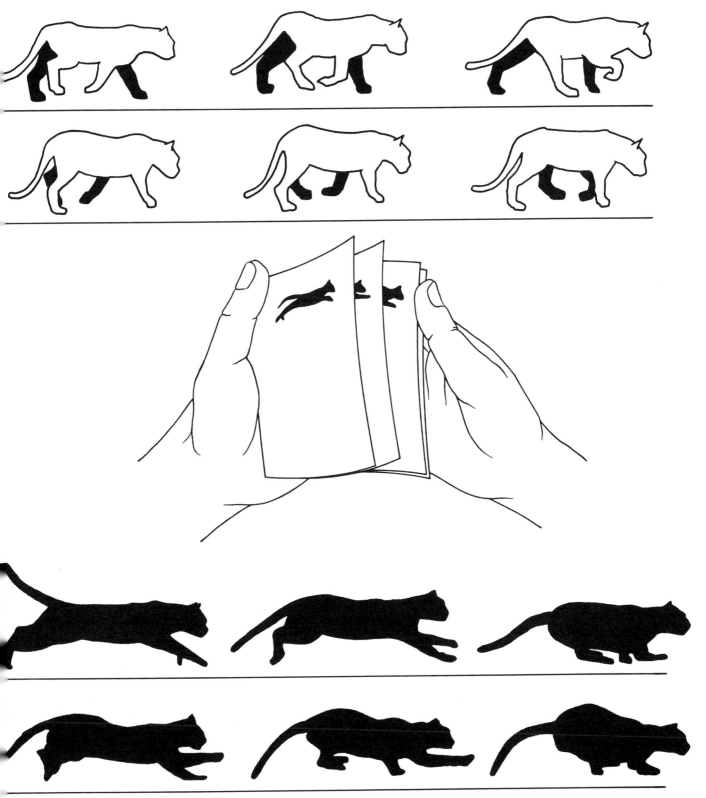

With X-ray eyes

If you had X-ray eyes, you would be able to
see the skeletons of all your friends and lots
of animals, too.

All skeletons are made up of a skull that
is the head and lots of bones that together
form the body.

On these pages, you can see the skeletons of
a rabbit, cow, cat, bat and mouse. Can you
tell which is which?

Can you name any creatures that do not
have skeletons?

Do butterflies or worms have skeletons?

Place tracing paper over one of the
skeletons and then draw an outline of the
creature's body with all its flesh and fur.

These skeletons are of animals in this book.
Turn to pages 50, 75, 77, 81 and 128 and
and compare the outside with the inside of
the animals.

Tin-can creatures

Sometimes it can be helpful to think of an animal's body as being made up from a collection of simple objects like balls, eggs, tubes, boxes or tin cans, just like those drawn here.

When you plan a tin-can drawing, remember that the legs on either side of the body are the same size. But if one leg is nearest to you, you will need to draw that one a bit lower and larger. This is true whether you are drawing a chair, a table... or an elephant.

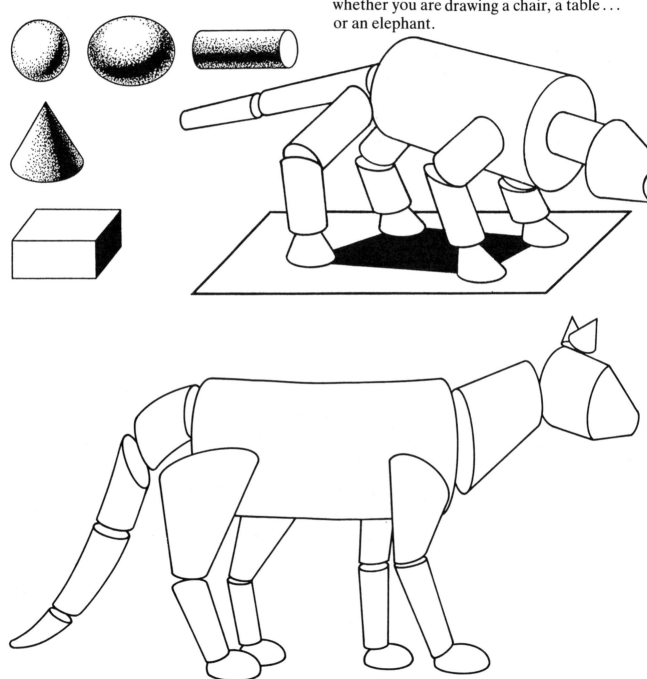

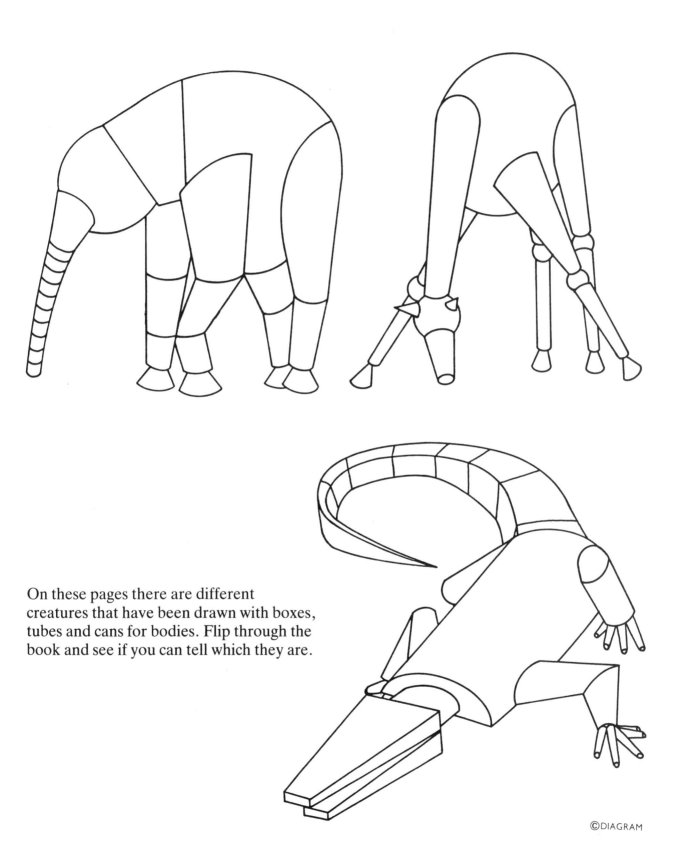

On these pages there are different creatures that have been drawn with boxes, tubes and cans for bodies. Flip through the book and see if you can tell which they are.

©DIAGRAM

Point of view

Animals often look rather different
depending upon where you look at them
from or your point of view.

If you saw him from above

If you stood in front of him

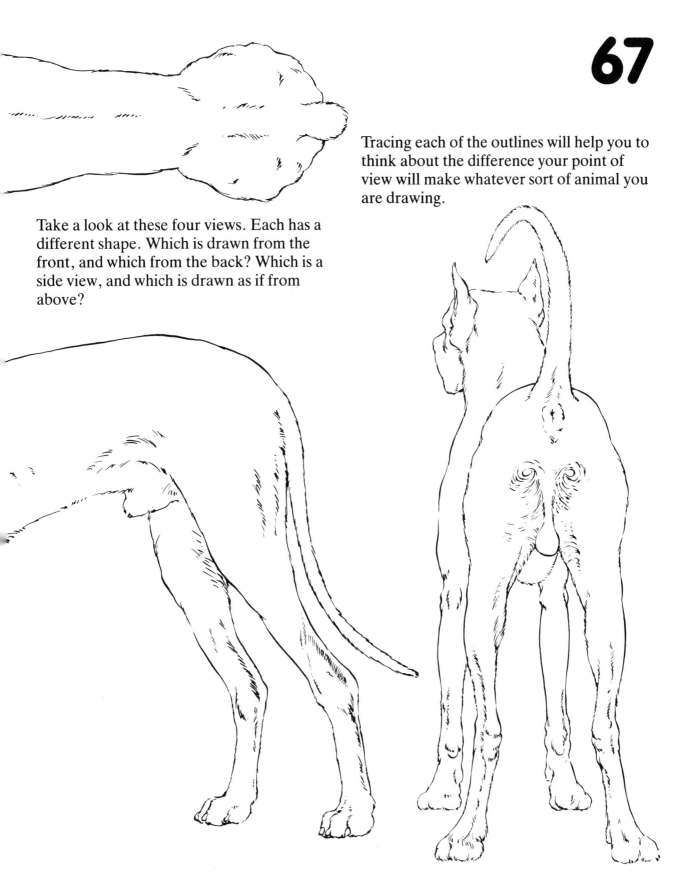

Tracing each of the outlines will help you to think about the difference your point of view will make whatever sort of animal you are drawing.

Take a look at these four views. Each has a different shape. Which is drawn from the front, and which from the back? Which is a side view, and which is drawn as if from above?

If you saw him from the side

If you stood behind him

©DIAGRAM

Part 4

Now it's time to start drawing lots of different animals that inhabit our planet. It is fun and easy to do in step-by-step stages, as you'll see.

In this part of the book, there are lots of drawings that you can trace and many you might like to copy, following the instructions carefully.

It will be best to use a soft pencil for planning your drawing.

The pages that follow show you how to construct your drawings. Of course, you can make them any size. But all the parts of the animals' bodies must be in proportion. This means that if the tail of an animal was the same length as its back leg, it must still be the same size as the back leg in a bigger drawing, too.

YOUR ANIMAL GALLERY

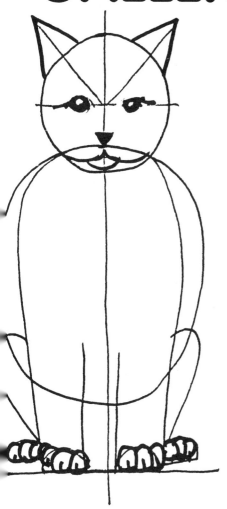

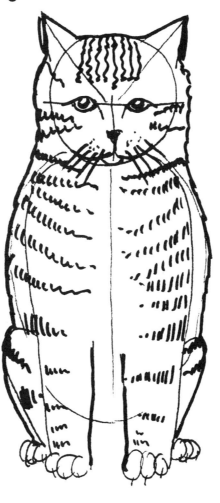

Follow the step-by-step stages shown here. You will notice that I have made some of the lines thicker than others. All **your** lines should be the same thickness. My thicker lines are just to show you what I have added at each step.

Prop up the book while you are drawing so that you do not need to keep opening it while you are copying and will not lose your page.

If you come to a part you find difficult, take your time. Draw slowly, and take care over all the detail.

Animal parade

Shown here are some of the creatures you will soon be drawing. All of them have been sketched from the side or the front. Notice how different they all are. Can you name them? Are there any you would love to have as pets?

There is another parade on pages 98–99, and then on pages 122–123 you'll find a final parade of unusual animals to draw.

©DIAGRAM

A sitting cat

These two pages show how you can draw a sitting cat from three different viewpoints – from the front, from the side and from the back. In step-by-step stages, build up your drawing using an oval for the body, a circle for the head and triangles for the ears. When you have finished the outline, you can then add texture for the cat's coat, which might be smooth like a Siamese or fluffy like a tabby.

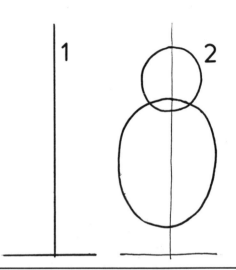

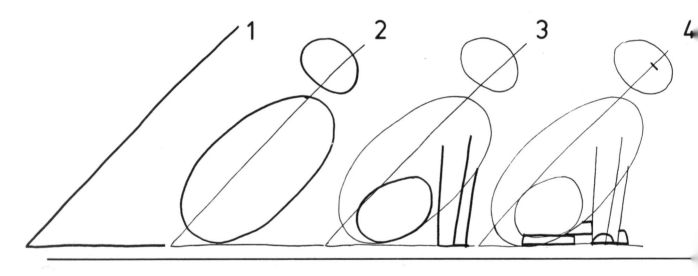

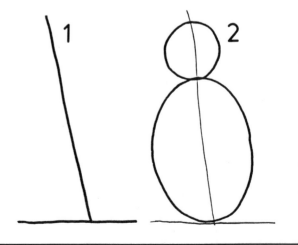

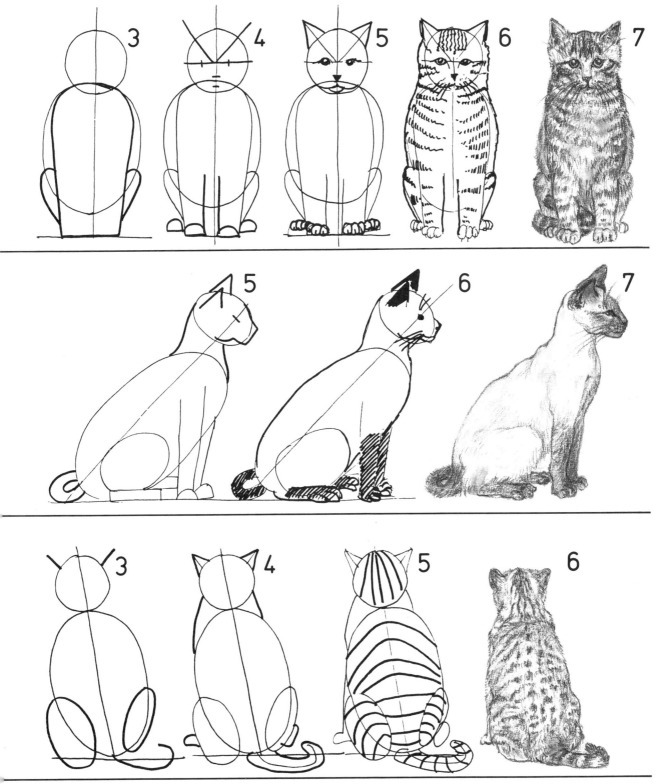

3 4 5 6 7

5 6 7

3 4 5 6

©DIAGRAM

A long-tailed mouse

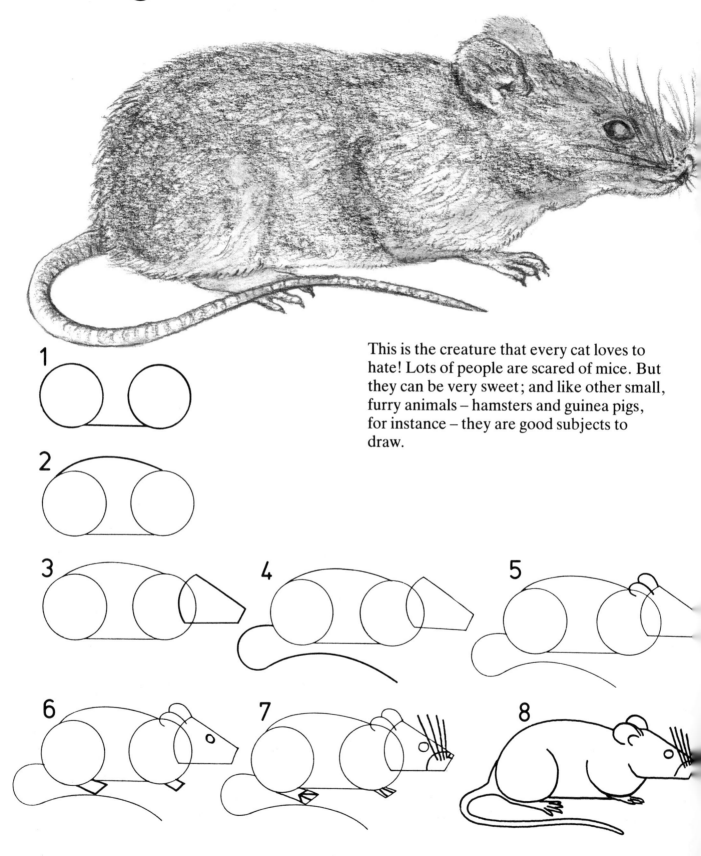

This is the creature that every cat loves to hate! Lots of people are scared of mice. But they can be very sweet; and like other small, furry animals – hamsters and guinea pigs, for instance – they are good subjects to draw.

Here are two views to copy. Again, you can build up your drawings using circles, ovals and a rounded oblong, with a wavy line for the tail. Use lots of short strokes for the body fur.

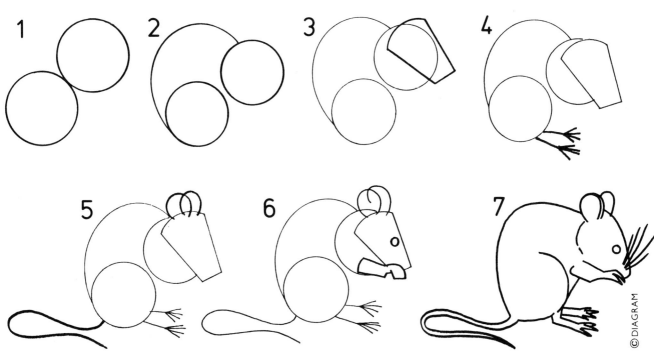

©DIAGRAM

A furry rabbit

This rabbit has been drawn in two positions
– lying down and sitting on its back legs.

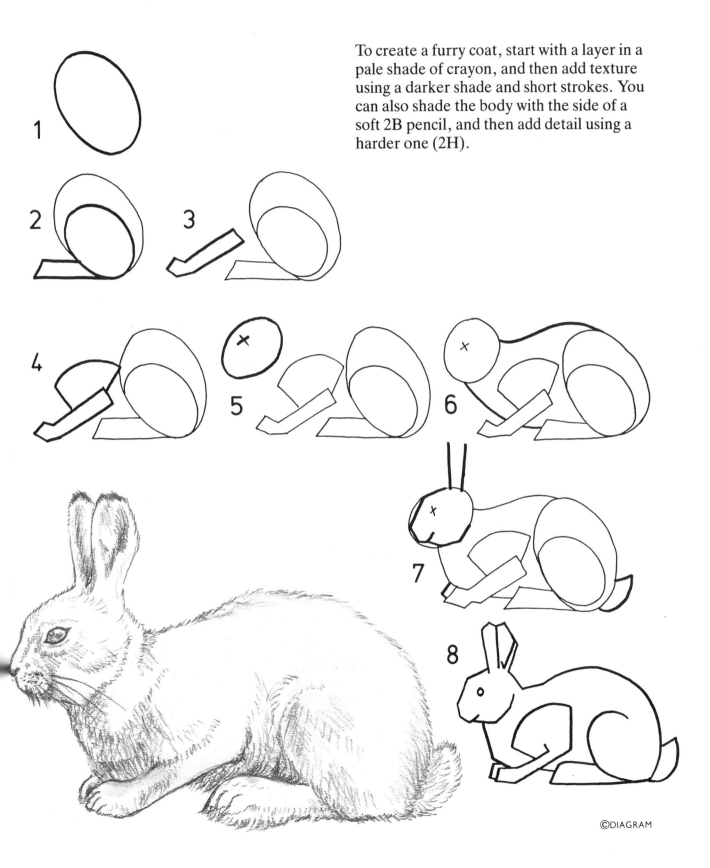

To create a furry coat, start with a layer in a pale shade of crayon, and then add texture using a darker shade and short strokes. You can also shade the body with the side of a soft 2B pencil, and then add detail using a harder one (2H).

1

2

3

4

5

6

7

8

©DIAGRAM

A handsome horse

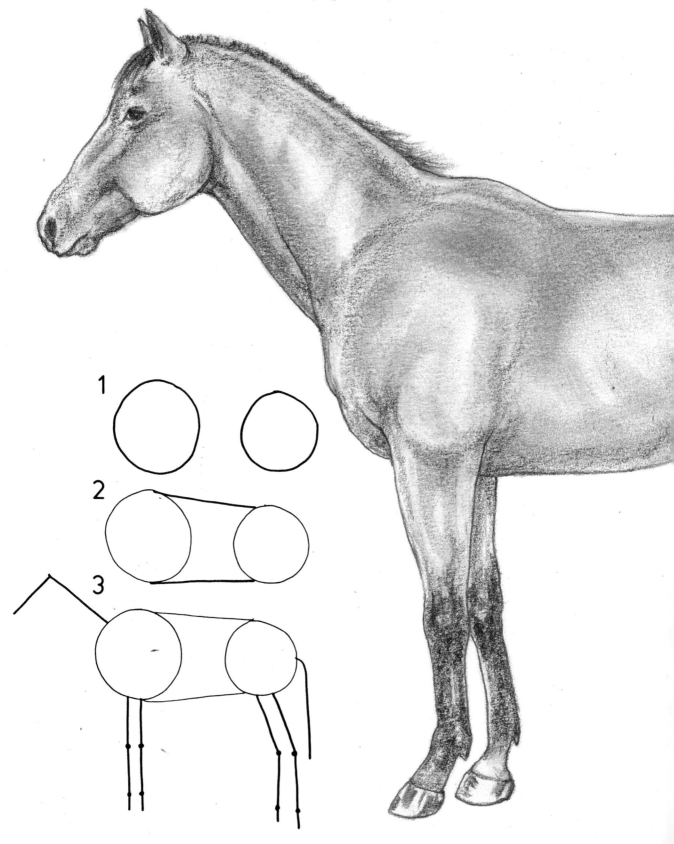

1

2

3

There are six simple stages to drawing the horse shown here. Follow them carefully, and you will find that our close friend is not as difficult to draw as you might at first think.

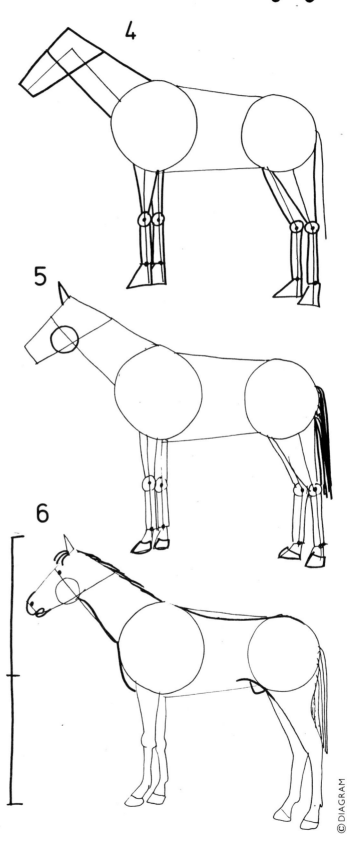

4

5

6

© DIAGRAM

A black and white cow

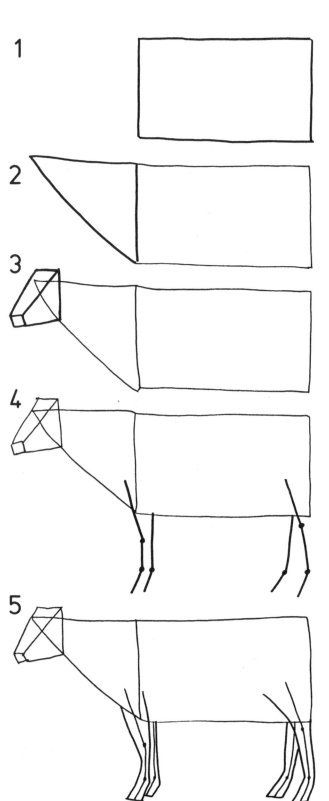

1

2

3

4

5

6

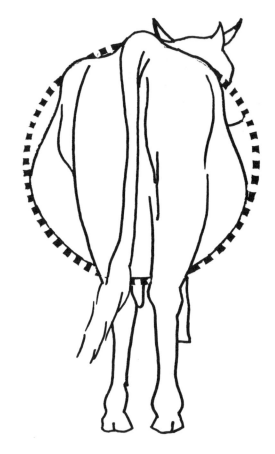

From the back, a dairy cow looks like a round barrel on legs. But from the side it has a more simple shape.

Begin with a box, as shown, and add a triangle at one end with another box (a bit like a pyramid on its side) for the head.

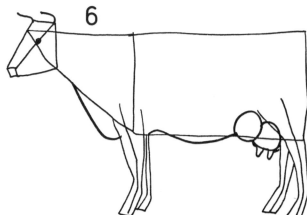

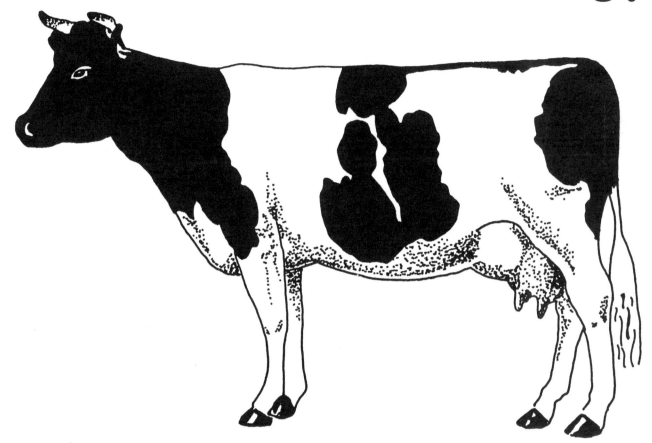

Next add stick legs, which you can round out. Then mark the position of the horns, the eye, the udder, the hooves and the tail. Finally, you can add its markings, using a thick pen to fill in the black areas, and a fine one to add the dots to shade the horns and belly. Look how straight the back is.

Don't forget to rub out your first pencil guidelines. Later, you could add a field where the cow could be grazing, and perhaps a tiny calf as well.

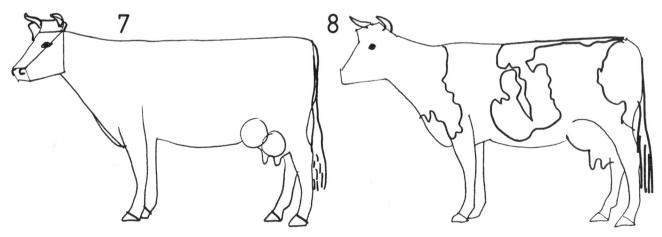

7

8

A piglet

This farmyard piglet is easy to draw because of its rounded body and funny snout. When you have finished your guidelines in pencil, you can go over them with brown crayon or felt-tips, and add details like the shiny black eye and lots of lines for the body hairs.

7

8

A spiky hedgehog

Start with an oval or egg shape, and then add a rounded triangle for the hedgehog's head before you start on details like the ear, nose, whiskers, eye and four tiny feet.

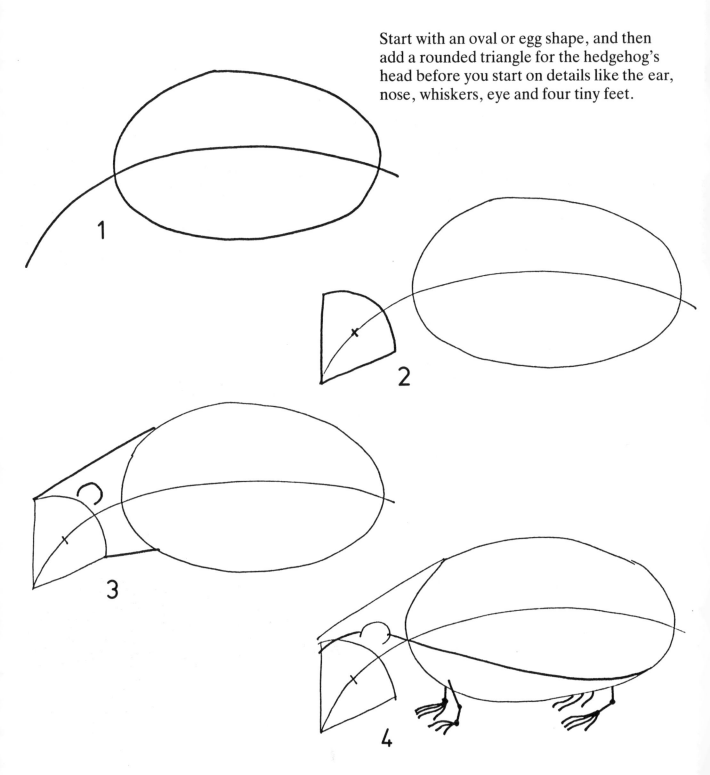

This is my son's drawing of a hedgehog which he says is very frightened.

5

When you add the spikes, remember to make them go in the same direction. If you draw lines on the belly with a sharp 2B pencil and work lightly, you will get a soft effect. For the spiky prickles, flick your pencil to make lots of heavy marks.

6

© DIAGRAM

A playful puppy

If you would like to copy this adorable
puppy, follow the step-by-step stages
shown.

This picture was done using crayon, but you
could also use felt-tips if you like.

Perhaps you have your own puppy, or know someone else with a young, playful dog. If so, your only chance of drawing this lively little animal is probably when it's asleep because it won't keep still when it's awake.

Cuddly kittens

Here are some kittens for you to start copying. Their shapes are like fluffy balls of fur. If you prefer, follow the step-by-step stages below, and remember to give them big, bright eyes.

1

2

3

4

5

Sheepdog

The great big ball of fur on the right is a lovely shaggy sheepdog with such long hair that it falls right over its eyes.

Underneath all that hair, however, it has a body that is not that different from the smooth Great Dane below.

To draw the sheepdog, start with a circle for the head and two oblongs for the body, adding two smaller circles for the front paws. You can then add rough lines for all the hair. Add a black, shiny nose and pink tongue. The eyes, of course, are hidden. What a cuddly pet!

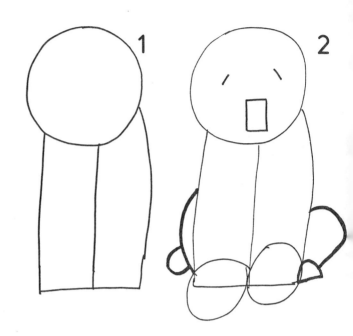

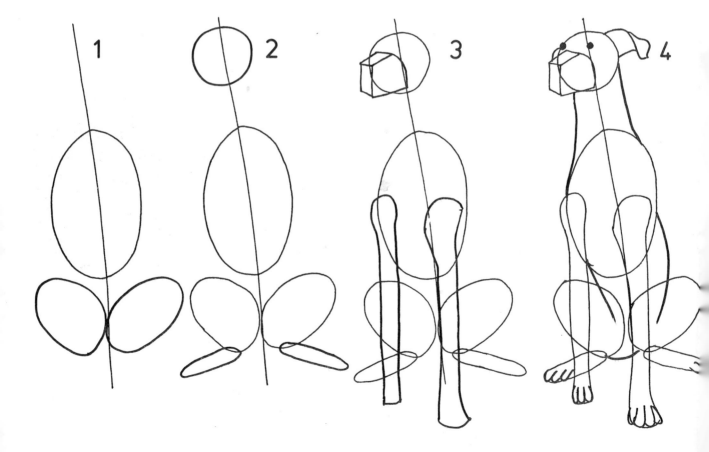

3

5

A bird in flight

This picture of a chaffinch in flight has been
copied from a superb photograph.

It may look complicated to copy, but if you follow the step-by-step stages, starting with a simple oval for the body, a circle for the head and a triangle for the beak, you should find it easier.

Make an arc for the wing, and then add the feathers like the sections of a fan. Make short strokes with a crayon, pencil or felt-tip for the feathers on the wings and tail.

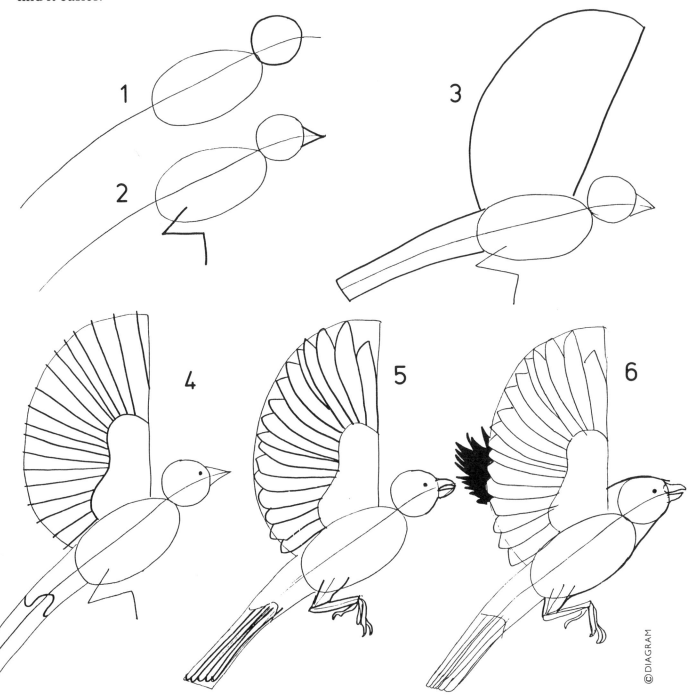

© DIAGRAM

A cat portrait

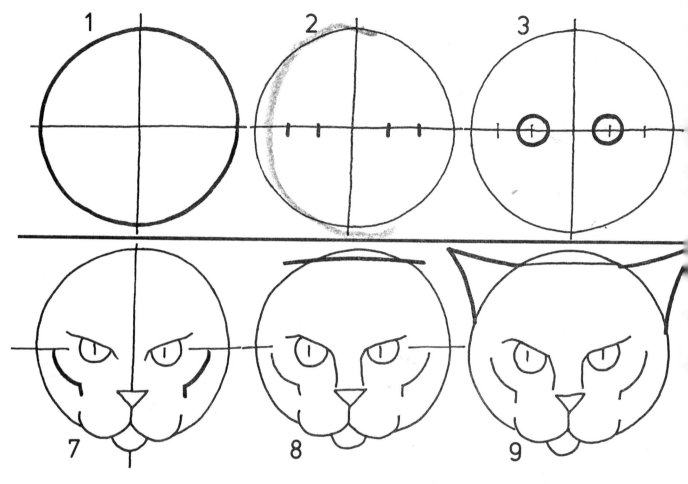

It can be fun just to draw an animal's face sometimes, putting in lots of detail.

Different breeds of cat have differently shaped faces. The face of a Siamese, for instance, is far more pointed than that of a tabby. But you can still start with a circle, and then add all the features. All your pencil guidelines that divide up the face can be rubbed out afterwards if you wish.

Take a look at the three faces at the bottom of the page. They all look very different, don't they? But each has big eyes, long whiskers and pointed ears.

A horse's head

These step-by-step stages show you how to develop a portrait of a horse's head from simple oblongs and box shapes.

For a front view, start with a simple rectangle which you can divide up into smaller ones to help you mark the positions of the eyes, nostrils and ears.

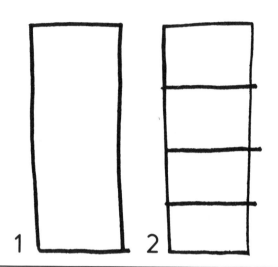

For the side view, start with this odd four-sided figure. Add a circle to mark the rounded part of the horse's jaw, and triangles for the ears. Mark dots where the nostril and eye will be.

For the final angle, think of the shape of the head as a long box. Again, divide this up into smaller boxes as shown, and pinpoint the position of the nostrils, eyes and ears. Then you can round off your basic guidelines and add detail.

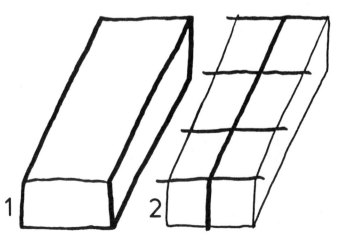

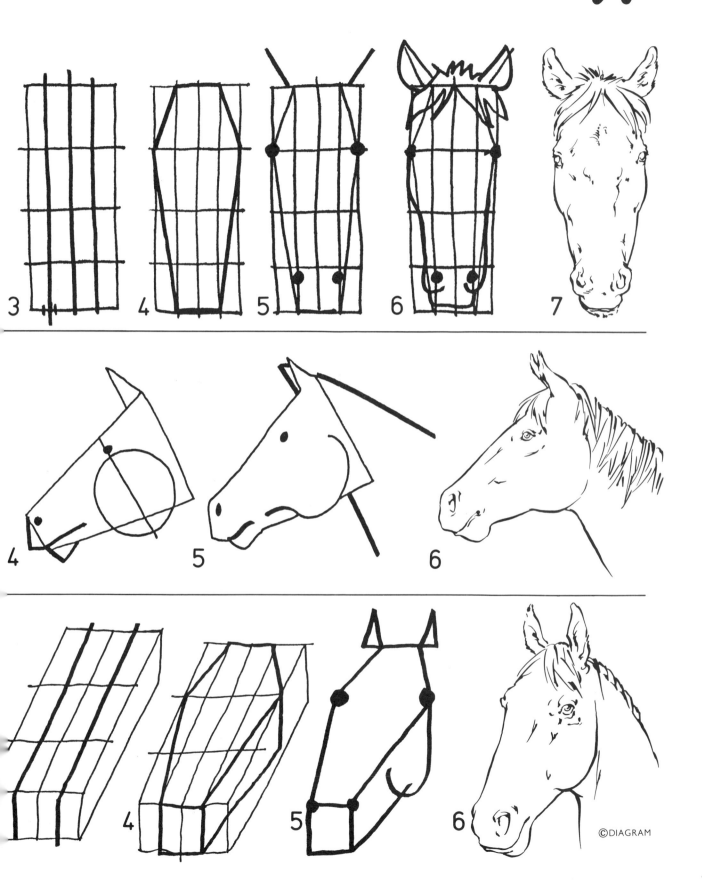

97

3

4

5

6

7

4

5

6

4

5

6

©DIAGRAM

The rough and the smooth

Take a look at the creatures shown here. Some have shells or scales. Others have fur or thick skin, and one has feathers. Can you name them all? Which would be softest to stroke, if it would let you?

The true wildlife artist takes great care over the texture of the creatures he or she is sketching. Lots of animals have patterned coverings – the tiger, giraffe and zebra, for example – and it is important to get these patterns right if you want your pictures to look realistic.

Wax crayons will help to give a rough or mottled effect. But a sharp pencil or fine pen will be best for details like feathers or scales.

Remember, too, that you can place your outlines over wood or fabric and get the effect of texture by rubbing with a soft pencil or crayon. Look back to pages 34–35 to find out how to do this.

An Indian elephant

Always the stars of zoos, circuses and safari parks, elephants are amusing to watch and to draw. Their great big bodies are basically large ovals, with smaller circles for the head, piles of boxes for the legs, and a long tube for the trunk.

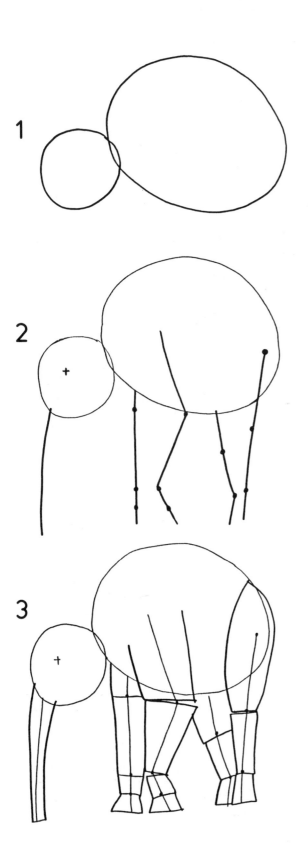

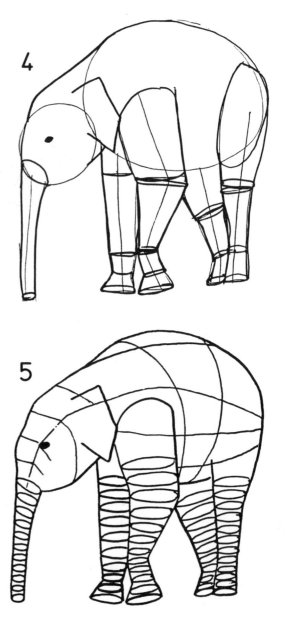

Give texture to the elephant's tough, thick skin by placing your outline over some glasspaper (sandpaper) or wood. Then rub over it with a soft pencil or wax crayon. You can add the wrinkles and creases on the legs and trunk using a sharp, hard (2H) pencil.

The long-necked giraffe

This long-legged, long-necked giraffe from Africa is bending down to sniff the ground. As you can see, its neck is just about as long as its legs.

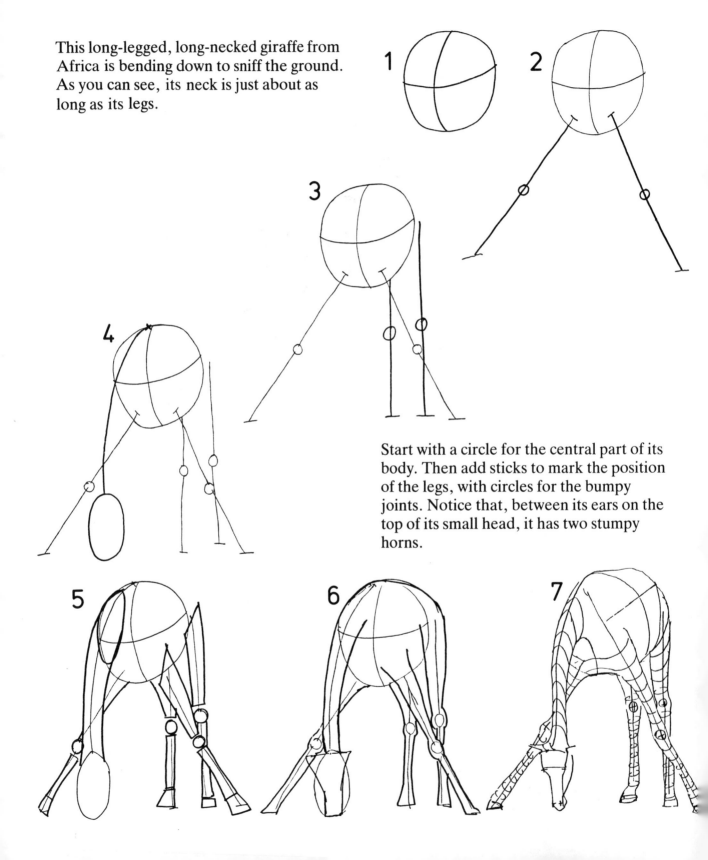

Start with a circle for the central part of its body. Then add sticks to mark the position of the legs, with circles for the bumpy joints. Notice that, between its ears on the top of its small head, it has two stumpy horns.

Once you have the outline, you can add the markings using either crayon, a soft pencil or brown water-based paint. Lots of animals have skin patterns like this to help them camouflage (say *cam-oo-flarge*) or hide themselves from other creatures who might want to attack them.

A striped zebra

With a similar shape to the horse on pages 78–79, this zebra has black and white stripes all round its body for camouflage in the long African grass.

Notice how the markings curve around the body and are not completely straight.

Build up this creature using a black felt-tip pen for the seven stages shown.

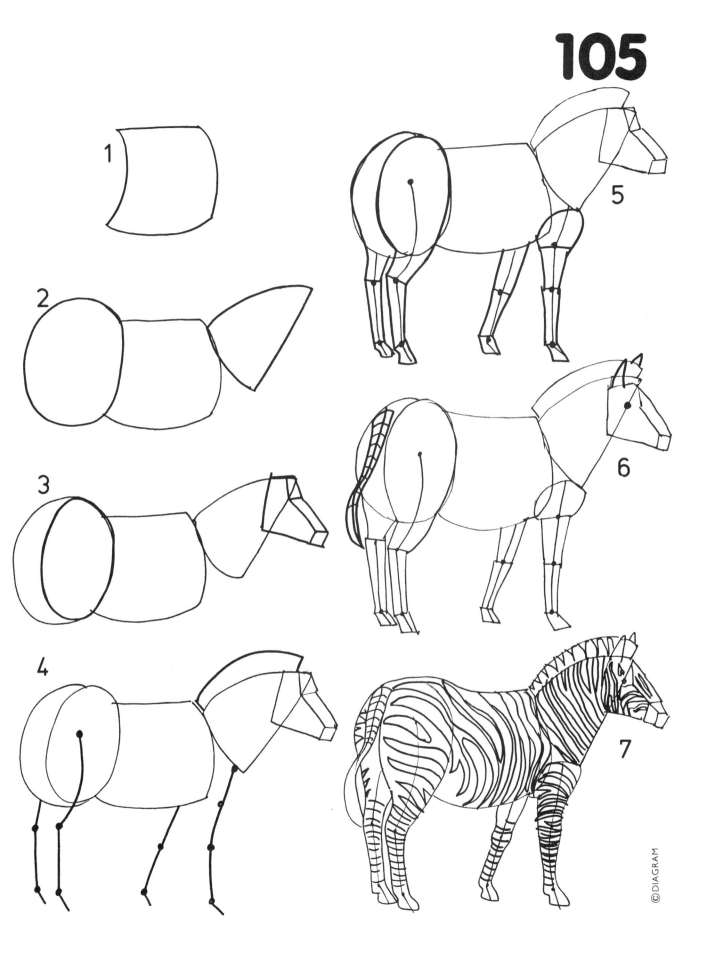

A terrifying tiger

Prowling through the dense forests of India, this magnificent man-eating tiger may look like a great big pet cat, but it is really terribly fierce.

Look at all the strength it has in its heavy body, long tail and sturdy feet!

1

2

When you have finished copying or tracing the outline of the body, shade it in brown and orange crayons and then add the skin markings in a darker brown or black. A tiger's stripes are not as clear as those on a zebra, remember.

How many other very large members of the cat family can you name?

©DIAGRAM

A lovable loris

This small cuddly creature is called a loris and is found in parts of Asia. It is an excellent climber and is nocturnal, which means that it is awake at night and sleeps by day. You might be able to see one at the zoo.

After you have made a rough outline, you can use lots of soft pencil strokes to give the effect of a very furry body. Perhaps draw two lorises climbing together.

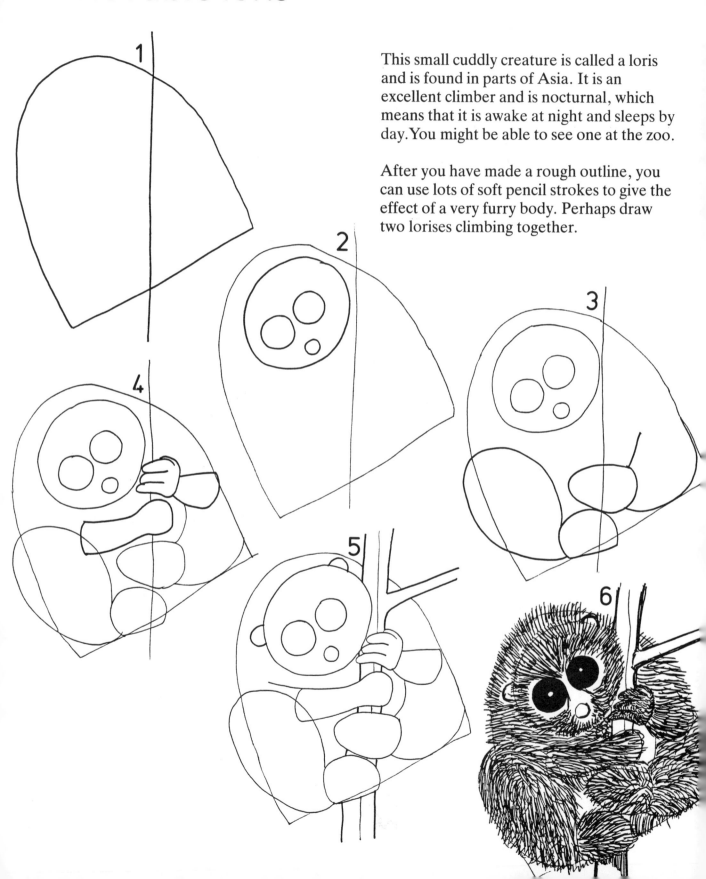

109

©DIAGRAM

A South American parrot

Once you have finished the parrot's outline, you can add the feathers and shade them to give texture. Notice that different parts of the parrot's body are covered in differently shaped feathers, and that they overlap in lots of layers.

You can see details of the feathers at the top of the next page.

Start with an oval, then add two wing shapes, one on either side. Place a small circle in the head position, add a hook for the beak, and a wide ring for the thick neck. The long claws are grasping a branch. Pretty Polly!

1

2

3

4

5

6

111

©DIAGRAM

A penguin

Penguins come from the continent of Antarctica around the South Pole. They always attract large crowds at the zoo.

Their bodies are smooth, but they also have feathers, which are quite different from those of the parrot on page 111. You can draw them using lots of short strokes. Remember to make the brush or pencil marks in the direction the feathers would grow – that means away from the body. If you press down with the brush, you will get a thick line. But if you lift the brush off your paper very carefully, you will get a thinner line. Leave the belly pale.

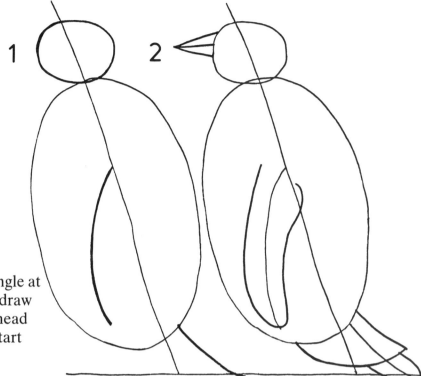

Begin by drawing a line to give the angle at which the penguin is standing. Then draw an oval for the body, a circle for the head and a banana shape for the flipper. Start the beak as a simple triangle.

©DIAGRAM

Fishy forms

Fish come in all sorts of shapes and sizes. Some are flat. Others are long and thin. Here are two for you to copy. The angelfish is thin and triangular, while the puffer fish can be as fat as a football.

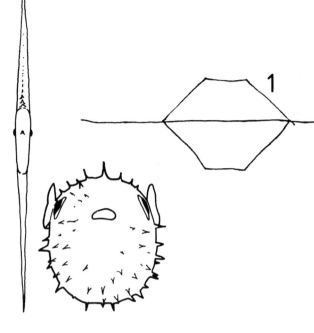

Here, above, are front views of a puffer and an angelfish. This is what they would look like if they were coming towards you. Can you tell which is which?

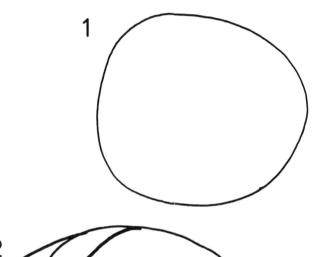

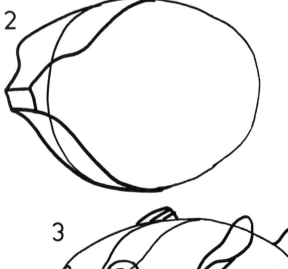

This deep-sea puffer gets its unusual name because it can puff itself up to twice its size to frighten away its enemies.

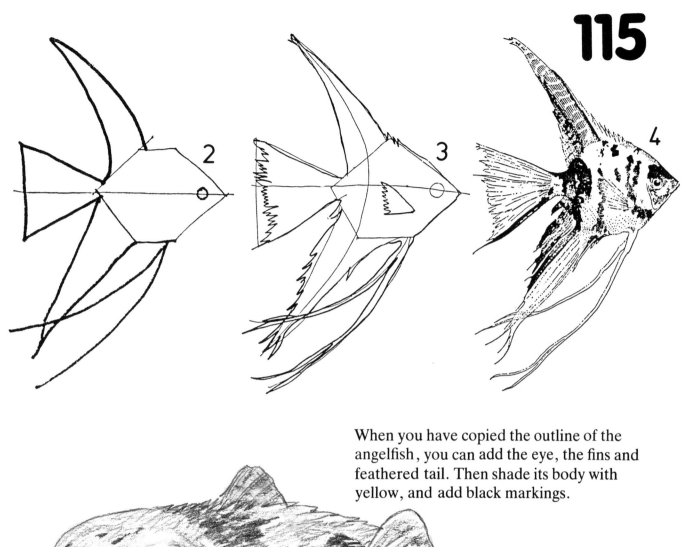

When you have copied the outline of the angelfish, you can add the eye, the fins and feathered tail. Then shade its body with yellow, and add black markings.

©DIAGRAM

A South American armadillo

The armadillo lives in the warm grasslands or pampas of the Americas. It has a tough outer covering that protects it from attack, and can also roll up into a ball to defend itself or burrow into the ground if an enemy approaches. Some are as long as you are tall; others are just the length of your hand.

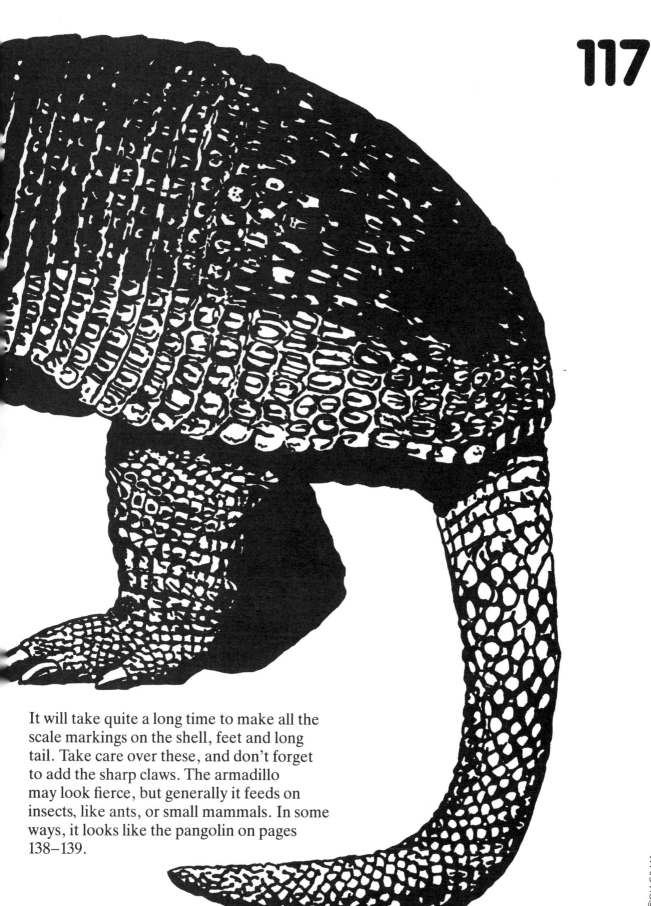

It will take quite a long time to make all the scale markings on the shell, feet and long tail. Take care over these, and don't forget to add the sharp claws. The armadillo may look fierce, but generally it feeds on insects, like ants, or small mammals. In some ways, it looks like the pangolin on pages 138–139.

Tortoises and turtles

These creatures have a large bony shell, under which they can pull back their heads when danger threatens. Most tortoises spend all their time on land, but some turtles are entirely aquatic – which means that they spend nearly all their time in the water.

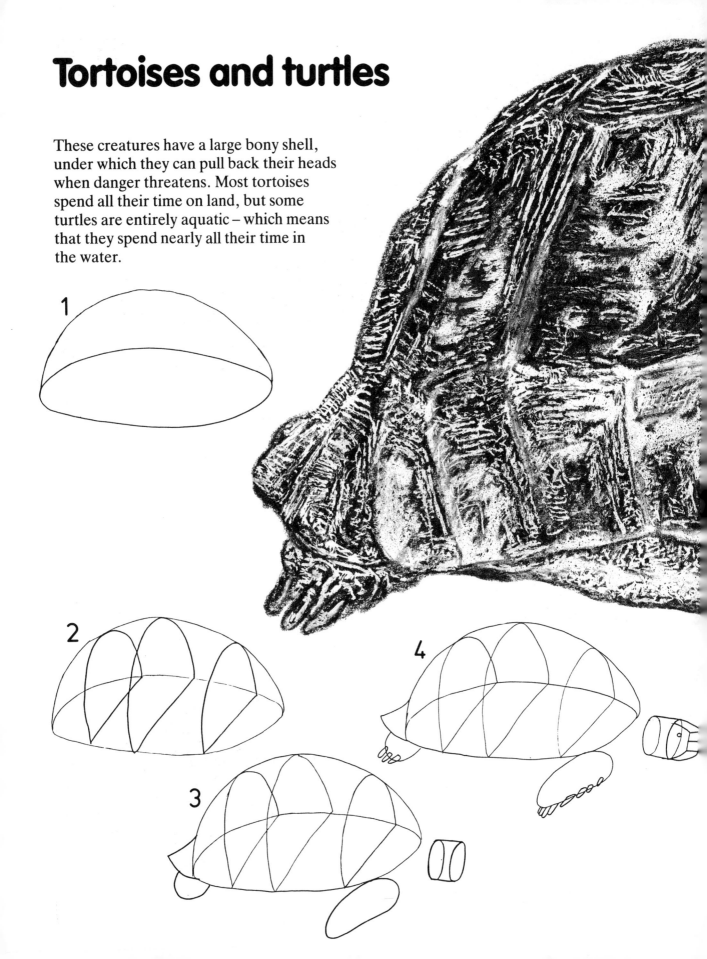

This tortoise looks unhappy, but only because of the shape of its mouth when it is closed.

Once you have drawn the basic outline, you can use the scratch and scrape method described on page 35 to make the shell pattern.

5

6

© DIAGRAM

An angry alligator

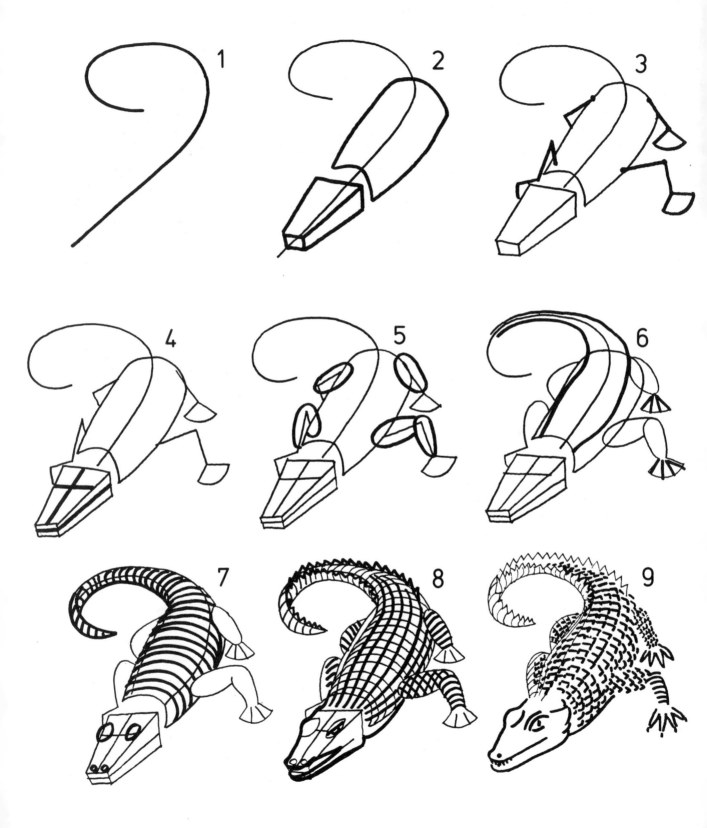

Alligators, with their enormously long tails, are much like crocodiles, and are so big and powerful that they can kill and eat an animal as big as a cow with just a few snaps of their huge jaws.

Build up this very fierce creature in the nine steps shown and then add its rough hide. You can give texture to your drawing by rubbing with a soft pencil over a rough surface like a brick. Don't forget to add its very sharp teeth. Watch out – there's an alligator about!

©DIAGRAM

Another animal parade

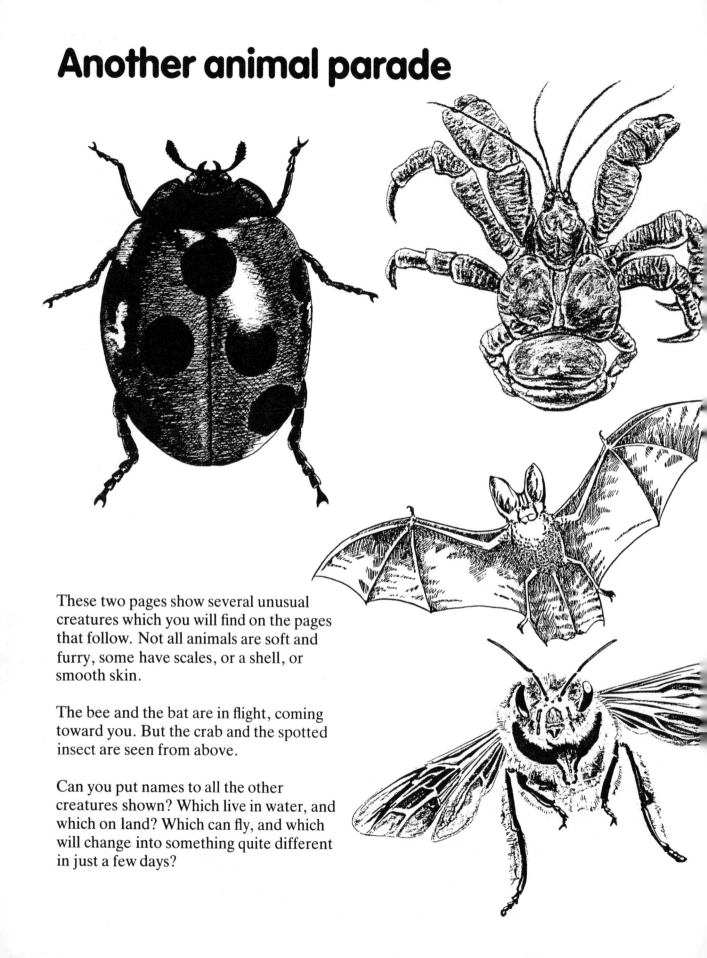

These two pages show several unusual creatures which you will find on the pages that follow. Not all animals are soft and furry, some have scales, or a shell, or smooth skin.

The bee and the bat are in flight, coming toward you. But the crab and the spotted insect are seen from above.

Can you put names to all the other creatures shown? Which live in water, and which on land? Which can fly, and which will change into something quite different in just a few days?

A seven-spotted insect

Americans call this insect a ladybug. (The British call it a ladybird – but it isn't a bird, and it might be male or female!)

It has been drawn from above so that its body looks almost perfectly symmetrical – in other words, the left half looks just the same as the right.

Make sure that you also draw each half to look the same, and that you put in all the parts that make up the six spindly legs.

Notice that the body is not completely flat but looks a bit like an upside-down bowl.

The outline can be drawn with a fine felt-tip, and the body dots filled in with a thicker pen or brush.

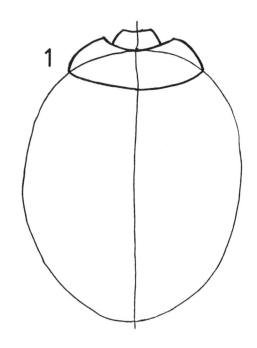

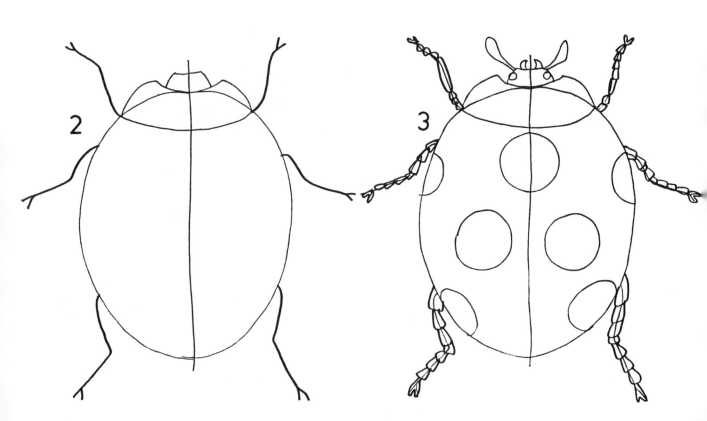

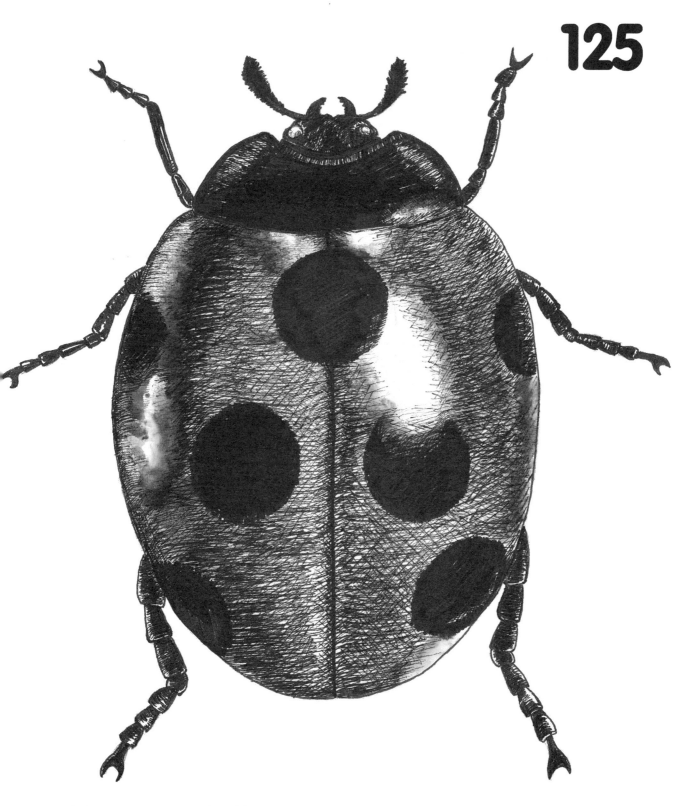

Most of these insects are red and have seven
black spots. They are usually smaller than
your little fingernail and live on other insects
like the greenfly.

Here it is at life-size!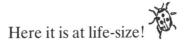

A robber crab

This giant robber crab is really about twice the
size of an adult human hand. It is the largest
of all land crabs, and can even climb trees
and cut down coconuts with its
enormous pincers.

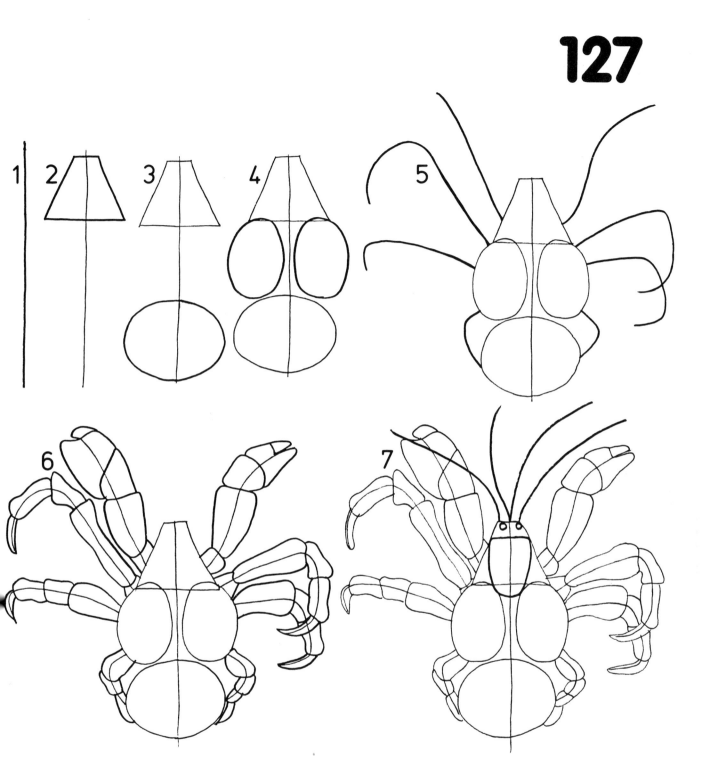

Look how many different parts there are to its body! The first stage in the step-by-step drawings is to sketch what looks like a lampshade, as shown. Then add three ovals, and next position the limbs.

Gradually add more and more detail. You can give texture to its rough shell by placing your drawing paper on a piece of wood and rubbing with a soft (2B) pencil.

©DIAGRAM

Flying bats

Bats do not look symmetrical when hanging asleep upside down, screeching down like dive-bombers or flapping their wings.

Here are bats in all sorts of positions which you can trace or copy.

If you have never seen a real-life bat, this may be because they only come out at night, when they feed on creatures like moths and beetles, fish and fruit, or even the blood of animals. Notice how the bat's wings are attached to its legs. They really are rather scary creatures, aren't they?

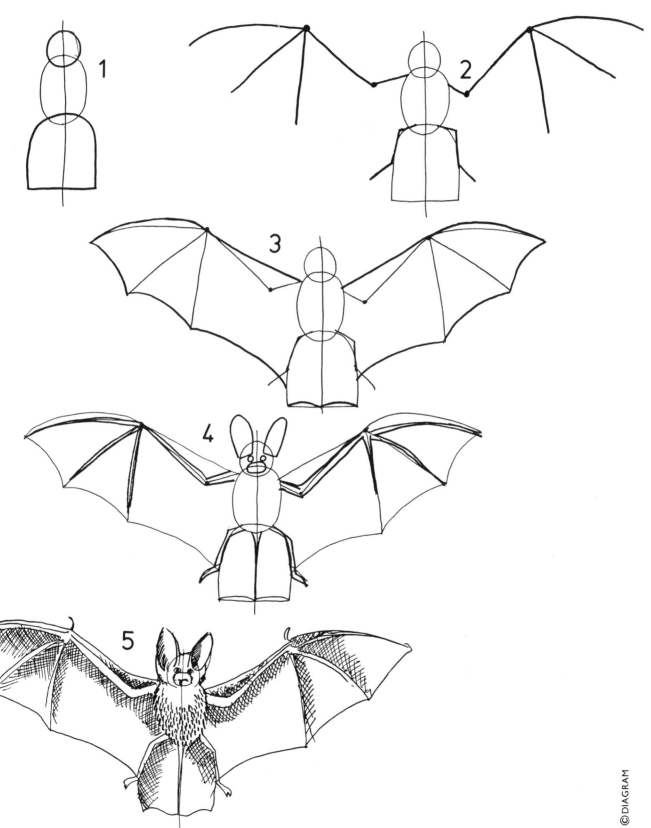

1

2

3

4

5

As busy as a bee

The step-by-step stages will help you to draw this bee in flight. Graham drew it with thin water-based paint so that the wings look almost transparent. It looks so life-like, it might just sting you!

Bees are among the busiest of all insects, making the honey we all enjoy by collecting nectar from flowering plants and returning with it to the hive where many hundreds of them live together.

It can be fun to draw a bee like this one on cardboard, and then cut it out and make a mobile to hang up. Your family and friends might just think it is a real bee!

©DIAGRAM

A tiny seahorse

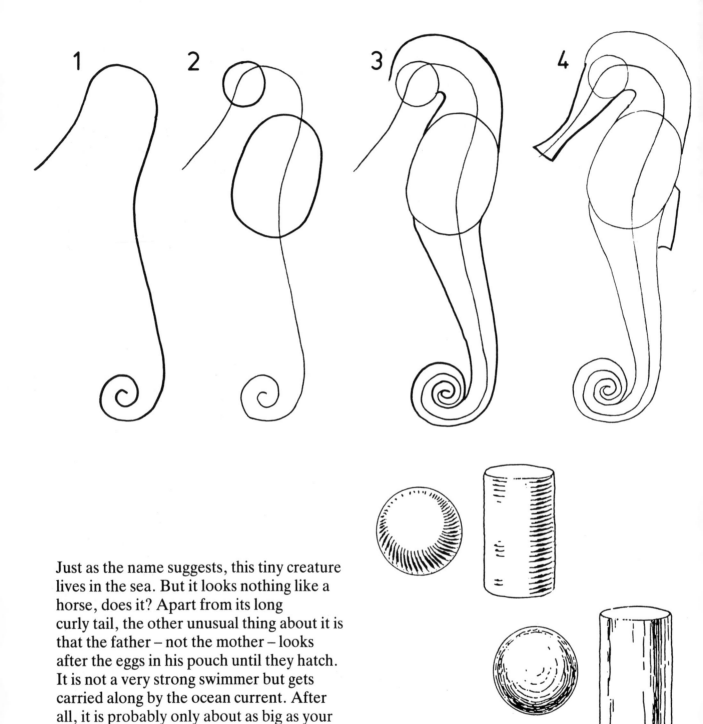

1 2 3 4

Just as the name suggests, this tiny creature lives in the sea. But it looks nothing like a horse, does it? Apart from its long curly tail, the other unusual thing about it is that the father – not the mother – looks after the eggs in his pouch until they hatch. It is not a very strong swimmer but gets carried along by the ocean current. After all, it is probably only about as big as your little finger.

Why not draw a whole underwater scene? You could include the fish on pages 114–115.

When you use a pen or felt-tip, you cannot make your drawing have soft, fuzzy tones. A felt-tip will just make marks, so you

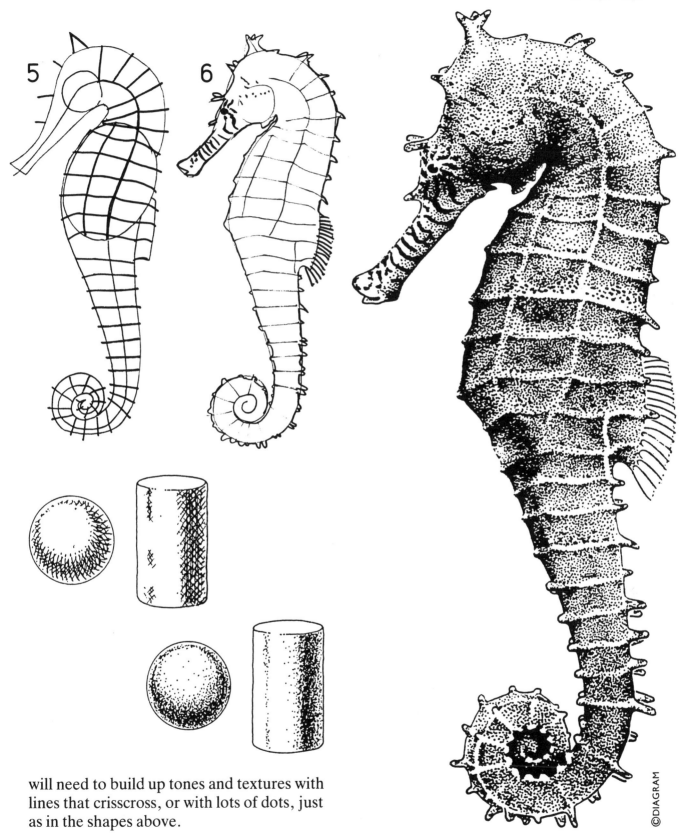

will need to build up tones and textures with
lines that crisscross, or with lots of dots, just
as in the shapes above.

Two leaping frogs

What you draw with will affect what your drawings look like. Here is Mary's drawing of a frog. She used a felt-tip and made lots of dots for the shading. Opposite is Jamie's drawing.

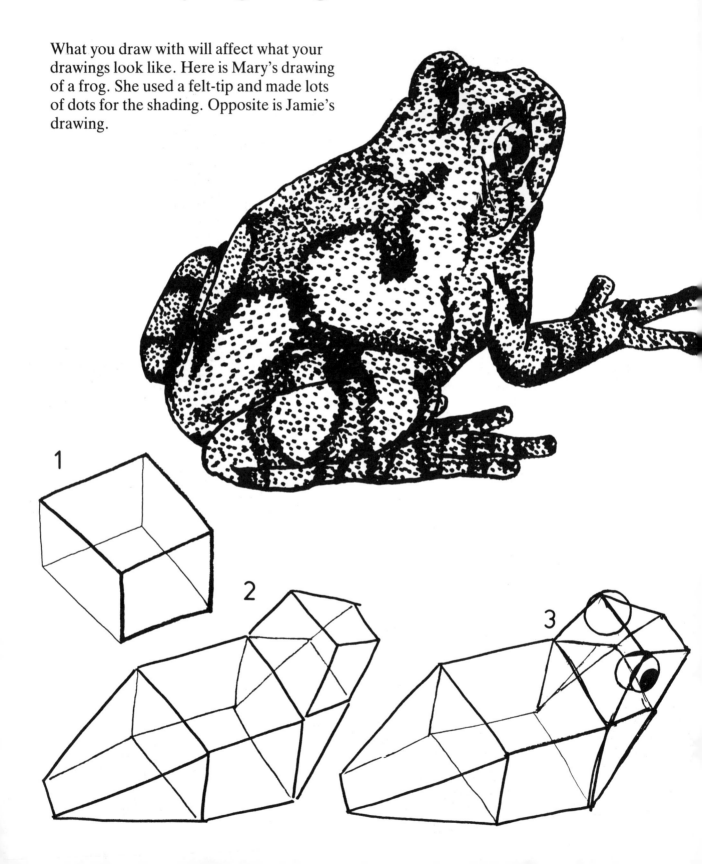

1

2

3

Jamie drew this frog on thin paper with a
felt-tip. Then he added some water with a
brush for the skin markings. You might like
to trace his drawing and then add your own
patterns to the skin.

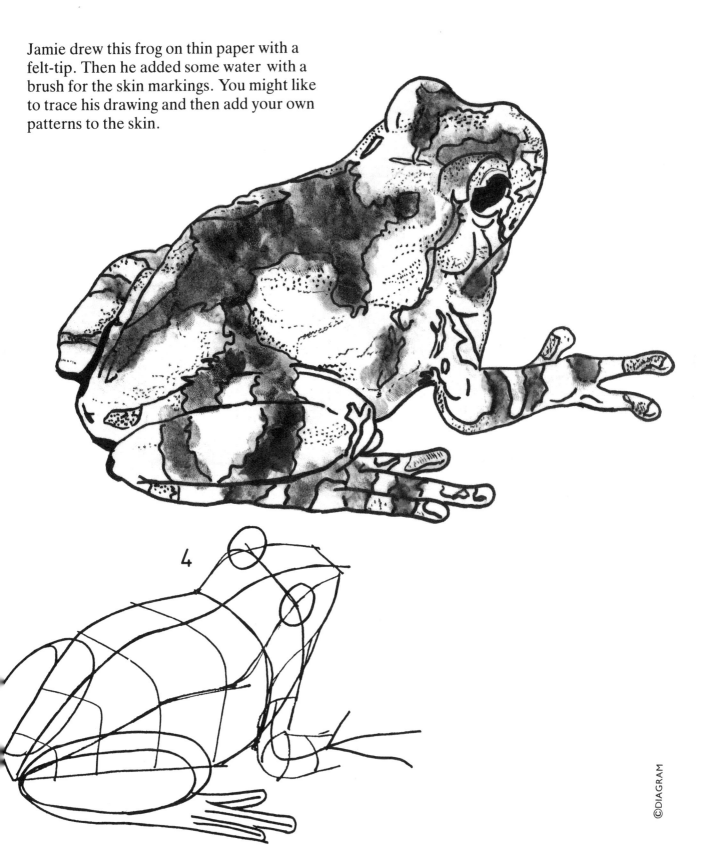

A caterpillar

This creature is very easy to draw.
As you can see, it is made up of lots of
segments or bits. Some caterpillars are plain
green but this one has spots. This helps it to
camouflage itself among leaves and hide
from other creatures that might be tempted
to eat it.

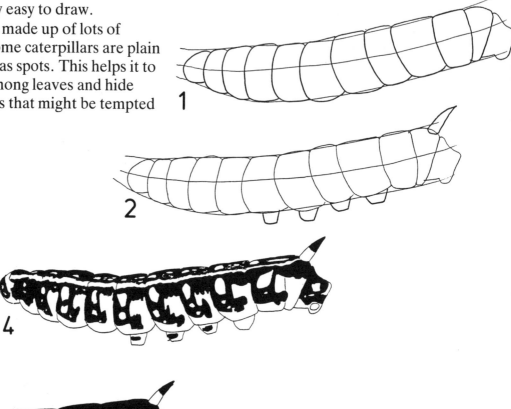

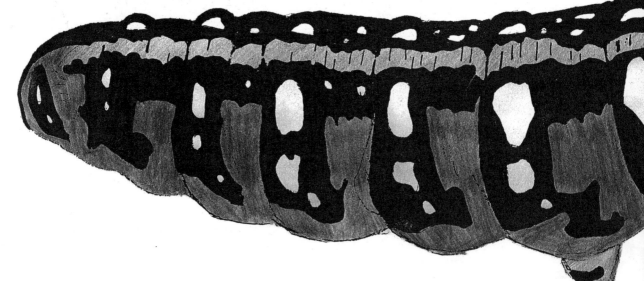

Trace the outline of the caterpillar and then add your own camouflage patterns using reds, blues, greens, browns, yellows and lots of other shades, too.

3

The caterpillar wriggles along twigs and branches, and will finally turn into the beautiful hawk moth shown. Other caterpillars turn into butterflies, of course.

©DIAGRAM

A pangolin

1

2

3

This very strange creature lives in Africa. It is covered by what looks like a suit of armour made up of large scales which overlap rather like a bird's feathers.

Notice how small its head is but that it has an extremely long nose and a big, wide tail, as well as clawed front limbs.

You can trace or copy the outline given here and then add your own scales and shading. Remember that the underneath should look darker because it is away from the light.

4

5

©DIAGRAM

These squares can be used for enlarging your drawings as shown on pages 44–45.

Index

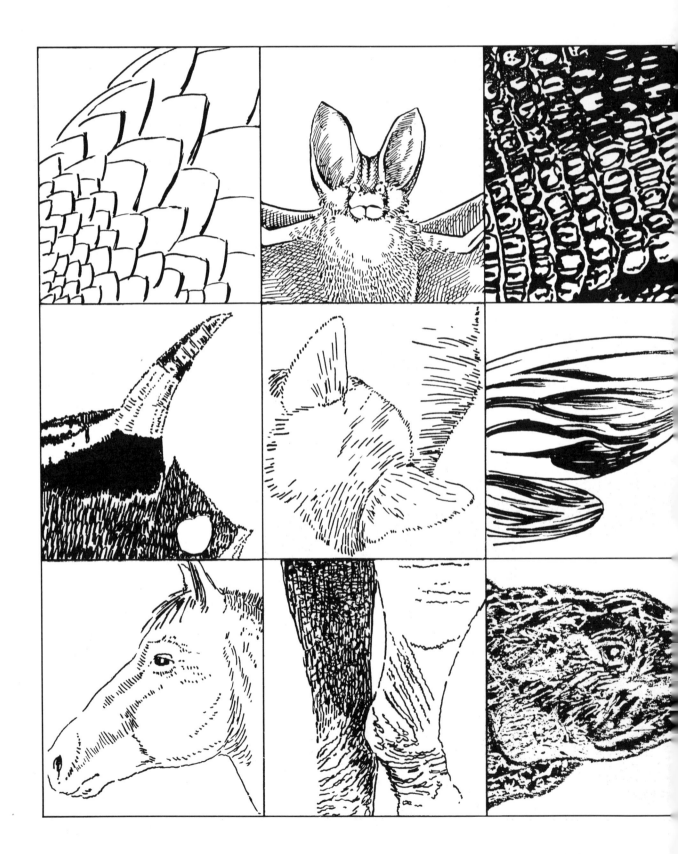

Here and at the front of the book are details
from some of the drawings featured. Can
you find the pages on which they appear?